THE LAST SITTING

THE LAST SITTING

BERT STERN

TEXT WITH ANNIE GOTTLIEB

BLACK CAT

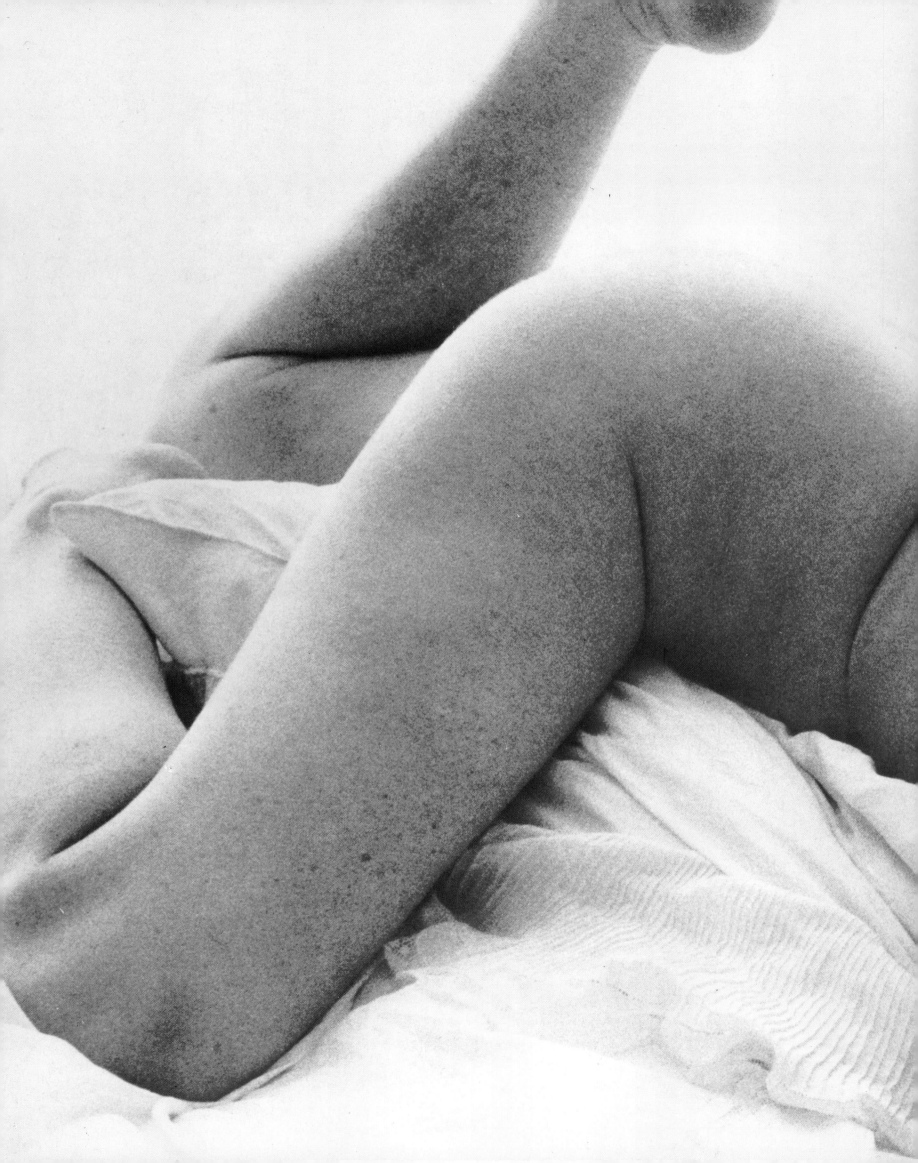

The author would like to thank Myroslawa Prystay for the instinct to contact Ned Leavitt of the William Morris Agency whose talent and devotion contributed so much to this book. Very special personal thanks to Pam Bernstein and Larry Chilnick for their invaluable support. To Sallie Baldwin and Brad Greene, thanks for their contribution to design and layout. Grateful thanks to the following: American Blueprint, Sherry Arden, Cheryl Asherman, John Ball, Michael Carlisle, Bryan Colmer, David Dalton, Joy Dermanjian, Oscar Dystel, Lidia Ferrara, Peter Fritz, Pat Golbitz, Larry Goldman, Rolf Gillhausen, Hotel San Regis, Larry Hughes, Michelle Lapautre, Gar Lillard, Erich Linder, Al Marchioni, Lynn Margileth, Modernage, Mondadori, Erik Mosel, Frank Mueller-May, Munchner Tiefdruck-Repro, Andrew Nurnberg, Lisa Queen, Pam Reid, Robin Richman, Jeff Sado, Dan Strone, Lothar Schirmer, Rhoda Weyr, and Hy Zazula Associates.

FOR ALLEGRA

The first time I saw her was at a party for the Actors Studio, in New York City. It was 1955. A friend and I had been invited, and when we walked in, there she was: Marilyn Monroe.

She was the center of attention. All the men were around her, and all the light in the room seemed focused on her. Or was the light coming *from* her? It seemed to be, because she glowed. She had that blonde hair and luminous skin, she wore a gleaming sheath of emerald-green that fit her body like a coat of wet green paint.

"Look at that dress," I said to my friend.

"I hear they sew her into it," he said.

How would you get her out of it, I wondered, with a razor blade?

I'd laid eyes on Marilyn Monroe only moments before and already ideas about taking her clothes off were going through my mind.

I walked toward her, not with any intention of speaking to her, just in a trance of pure attraction. I had about as much control over myself as a moth flying around a candle. I wasn't more than three or four feet away when she turned and smiled in my general direction, her dress shooting green stars. I was dazzled. I didn't question why she would be smiling at me. At that instant I fell under her spell. It was a moment I wanted to go on forever.

I stopped transfixed where I was, on the edge of the crowd.

At that time I was a photographer and a pretty good one at that. Anyway that's what people told me, and there must have been something to it because I was getting a lot of work in advertising. I took audacious pictures that got people to want things. To illustrate the caption "Driest of the Dry" for Smirnoff Vodka, I had gone all the way to Egypt to photograph a dry martini in front of a pyramid. And I had positioned the shot so that an image of the pyramid appeared upside down in the martini glass. I thought the trip was worth it. And Smirnoff wasn't hurting either. That year their sales skyrocketed, and that wasn't so easy for a vodka with a Russian name in the cold war fifties.

For a kid from a medium-poor Brooklyn family, I was on my way. But compared to Marilyn Monroe, I was still nobody. And I was shy. It was easier for me to fly halfway around the world for one ad shot, than to walk up to her and say, "Hi. I'm Bert Stern. I'd like to take your picture."

It did occur to me that she looked easy to love.

She laughed in the center of her circle of light and men. I stood in the dark, in the shadows, and I watched. And wanted.

And then I left.

I didn't dream that I'd ever get any closer to her than I was that night.

In 1962, things were different.

I was beginning to realize that the American dream machine really existed. For me it took the shape of a camera. As long as I carried one around it was amazing what I could get, and *who* I could get. A lot of my wildest dreams were beginning to come true.

I had become a *Vogue* photographer. That had been my dream ever since I first held a camera in my hands. I had fallen in love with photography at eighteen by opening an issue of *Vogue* and seeing a color still life by Irving Penn. For me, *Vogue* represented not only the best in photography, but a chance to take photographs of beautiful women. In the fifties and early sixties, believe it or not, you weren't allowed to show women in liquor ads. I guess the combination of sex and alcohol was considered too explosive. But women and photography were the two things I loved most in the world, and when I

became a *Vogue* photographer, I got my chance to combine them.

I was a success at *Vogue*. My pages sold clothes. I thought it was because my pictures were about the women under the clothes. But whatever the reason, *Vogue* had given me a contract to shoot one hundred fashion pages a year. And on top of that, I got ten pages to do whatever I wanted with—and enough expense money to produce them.

It was an ideal job. And I was still doing all the ads for Smirnoff. I could make as much as $10,000 in a week shooting for them. On top of that I'd just gotten a call from 20th Century-Fox, asking me to be the exclusive photographer for *Cleopatra*. The movie starring Liz Taylor and Richard Burton was about to start shooting in Rome. They agreed to fly me back and forth as often as necessary and to put me up in the Grand Hotel. So you could say I wasn't doing badly as a photographer.

Personally I was doing pretty well too. In 1959 something had happened that made it all perfect. That was the year Marilyn Monroe came out in *Some Like It Hot*. It was also the year I married the girl of my dreams—a girl I had fallen in love with at first sight on a Broadway stage.

Her name was Allegra Kent. She was a ballerina, a fabulous creature who brought tears to my eyes in *Swan Lake* and made my blood boil in *Cage*. She was talented, beautiful, and disciplined. She had high standards, and in some ways being her husband was the toughest assignment of my life. We'd already been separated once, but were back together again, and I was a happy man. We even had a little baby.

So, in 1962, I was trying to think where you go next when you have everything. I wasn't totally satisfied with my work at *Vogue* and I wanted to push myself further. I'd shot a lot of good pictures for them, but nothing that really measured up to that pyramid picture I'd done for Smirnoff. Now I wanted to take that mixture of adventure, optics and myth and apply it to photographing beautiful women.

I had those ten pages in *Vogue*. And what I wanted to do was put an image on those pages that would be delicious—and utterly memorable. What could be more challenging or mysterious than the pyramids?

A woman. It had to be a woman.

Making love and making photographs were closely connected in my mind when it came to women. Not that I made love to the women I photographed—but if I wanted a woman, a photograph was a very special way of having her.

Marilyn Monroe.

A beautiful picture of Marilyn Monroe in *Vogue . . . that* was an idea that had a glow to it. I was almost certain that *Vogue* had never run a photograph of her. Richard Avedon had done a spread of her in *Life* using lush, expensive sets. I thought they were great show-biz pictures, but they weren't exactly intimate. They didn't give any feeling of who *she* was. The definitive picture of *her* had still to be taken—one immortal black-and-white photograph—like Edward Steichen's portrait of Greta Garbo. That was the only picture I considered a great photograph of a movie star. And there was *no* picture of Marilyn Monroe that came close to being as good.

It sounded like a dream job.

On the plane to Rome I felt that I was going the wrong way. Toward the brunette, away from the blonde. Blondes have always been the escape route for me; brunettes *scare* me. The darker the woman, the more I've wanted to escape, enjoyed escaping. The lighter the woman, the more I've run toward her, escaped *with* her. And here I was, flying to Italy to photograph Elizabeth Taylor when the place I really wanted to be was in golden California with Marilyn Monroe.

Airplanes are great places to dream. I pushed my seat back, closed my eyes, and conjured up Marilyn's face.

I think that every man holds an image in his mind's eye of the woman who is the very incarnation of love for him. Marilyn Monroe was that magic image for me as she was for millions of other American men.

It wasn't love at first sight. The first time I saw her, I didn't think she was so great. I was sitting in the Kingsway Theatre, in Brooklyn, watching a movie called *The Asphalt Jungle.* There was a girl on the screen, and I thought, How did *she* get in the movies?

She didn't even look like a movie star to me. She looked like an ordinary girl who might have walked into the soda fountain down Kings Highway where I had worked as a soda jerk after school. She was only four or five years older than I was and she was up there on the screen. I was in the theater, in the dark, in Brooklyn, wondering, how'd she get that part? She must know someone. I'll bet she's the girl friend of somebody in Hollywood.

She was still only one step from Norma Jean Baker then—a nobody. To become the American dream girl, she had to dream herself up. And over the years I watched her do it. From movie to movie, I saw the dream develop, just like a photograph. That coloring . . . champagne, silver . . . she was creating herself, coming closer and closer to the pure power of Woman. Maybe she had to work hard at it, maybe it took hairdressers and makeup artists to keep her image up, but she *felt* it. She lived it. By the time I saw her at that Actors Studio party, she *was* her own creation.

The wish to photograph her must have begun way back then. Just the seed of an idea, waiting for its time. Now in 1962, I had enough confidence and self-respect as a photographer to tackle her. I had become enough of a master of my art—seeing—to match her mastery of the art of being seen. The time was ripe.

I knew she didn't agree to many photo sessions anymore. She and Arthur Miller were divorced now. Baseball player, Broadway playwright . . . she'd failed with DiMaggio, and now her second attempt to marry America had ended in tears. When I saw her in *The Misfits,* out in the desert screaming at the men not to hurt the wild mustangs, I thought, that's not just acting. She's fighting for her life.

The FASTEN SEATBELT sign flashed on and the pilot made some announcements in English and Italian. The plane was coming down in Rome. I had been thinking about Marilyn Monroe for hours and I said to myself, if you want something that badly, the best thing to do is ask for it.

I took a taxi straight to the Grand Hotel and walked into the lobby. Gilt and marble and mirrors, violin music playing in the next room . . . luxury always gives me courage. As soon as I got to my room I reached for the phone.

"Get me New York," I said, feeling a little like James Bond.

"Hi, boss!" Vickie, my girl Friday, answered the studio phone.

"Vickie, call Marilyn Monroe's agent and see if she'll pose for me for *Vogue.*"

"Oh, what a *great* idea!"

"And check it out with *Vogue.* Go over to their library and see if they've ever run a picture of her. Okay?"

"Will do."

I hung up, feeling that at least I'd set the wheels in motion.

The next morning I went over to the *Cleopatra* set. There were a lot of guys in battle uniforms standing around, and a photographer I knew was sitting on the floor outside Liz Taylor's dressing room, unshaven and half asleep. When he saw me, he looked up and said, "Hi, Bert! You going in there?"

I said, "Yep."

"Good luck," he said. "I've been waiting here for days to take her picture."

"Well, I'm not going to wait around," I said, and I walked in.

There was Elizabeth Taylor in the giant dressing room Fox had built for her, about a mile long. She was with Eddie Fisher, and the first thing she said was, "Gee, Eddie, doesn't he look like Mike Todd?"

I said to her, "I've come all the way from New York just to take your picture."

She said, "Oh, really?"

I said, "Yes, and I'd like to know when we're going to do it, because that's the only reason I'm here."

"Well!" she said. "You're pretty cocky, aren't you?"

"No, I'm not cocky," I said. "I'm here for you, and I'll stay as long as you want. But I just want to know *when* I'm going to photograph you. Tell me we'll do it in two weeks, and I'll come back and do it in two weeks. Tell me tomorrow, I'll do it tomorrow. Or the next day. It doesn't matter to me. But I am not going to sit around Rome for two weeks wondering when I'm going to do it."

She said, "How's tomorrow at ten?"

I said, "Great," and I left.

I got there the next morning at ten and set up my lighting. She said she was going to do her own makeup, which would take four hours. I said that was fine with me, because it would take me four hours to get the lights right. It was more like six hours before she was ready, but when she came out in her Cleopatra makeup, it was worth the wait. She was perfect, even with the scar on her throat from her recent tracheotomy.

I knew the picture right away.

She said, "What do you want me to do?"

I said, "You look fantastic. Just sit down, and *don't move.*"

She said, "That's all you want me to do?"

"That's it. Don't turn your head, look straight into the camera." And I just shot. I wouldn't let her move one inch. I made her stay in that position—straight on, locked in—and I shot the same picture over and over until I got it.

The phone rang while I was packing in my hotel room. It was Vickie in New York.

"Good news, boss," she said. "Yes, yes, and no. Marilyn Monroe says yes, *Vogue* says yes, and no, they've never done her before."

Sometimes I think there's such a thing as mind over matter. There's a force . . . you can call it intelligence, or consciousness, or you can call it magic. Whatever it is, it's everywhere. But the only way you can experience it is to get totally involved in something you love. Then, and only then, there's so much energy at work that a key may bend if you're Uri Geller, or you may get to meet Marilyn Monroe.

I've had that experience a few times in my life. Now, looking back, I sometimes wonder whether my own desires were the tools of something else—something that wanted to make children, or pictures, or trouble, for purposes of its own.

I got on the plane in a mood to celebrate. I settled down in my seat and ordered champagne.

It was all set. I'd proposed, and the girl had said yes. All I had to do now was take the picture.

I was going to do a head shot. One classic black-and-white photograph that would last forever. But if I was honest with myself, what did I *really* want?

To get Marilyn Monroe alone in a room, with no one else around, and take all her clothes off.

No one had gotten Marilyn Monroe to pose in the nude since Tom Kelley took those famous calendar shots. Pure Marilyn was what I wanted, and I didn't see what clothes had to do with it. Somehow getting her clothes off made the same kind of sense to me as going to Egypt to turn a pyramid upside down in a martini glass.

I just didn't see how I was going to do it.

Well, I'd worry about that later. First I had to decide *where* we were going to do it. Marilyn had set only one condition: the sitting had to be in L.A.

A downtown Hollywood studio didn't fit the bill at all. She would never take her clothes off in a rented studio.

In a hotel room, on the other hand . . .

I had it. The Bel-Air Hotel.

The Bel-Air is the most secluded, private, beautiful hotel in L.A. It's tucked away up in the hills of Bel-Air, and at first sight it looks Japanese. It has those artistic qualities of space and design, trees and flowers and quiet. There's a little bridge across to the entrance, swans in the pond down below, and a labyrinthine garden you could get lost in. It's really a fairy-tale environment—all arches, and pink stucco, and little courtyards full of flowers, and cool passageways down which discreet maids hurry with fresh sheets, and waiters with rattling carts of room service. It's a sexy hotel. Every room has a fireplace and every room is placed to give maximum privacy.

I didn't know that Marilyn knew and loved the hotel. She actually lived there off and on in between various husbands, and now she was on her own again. It would make sense, meeting me at the Bel-Air. She would feel at home.

Back in New York I felt a little like a man planning his wedding and honeymoon. I was going to photograph Marilyn Monroe. All I had to do was figure out how to get what I wanted: pure Marilyn, nude. But I didn't know how to approach her with that idea. I certainly couldn't just walk up to her and say, "Hi, my name's Bert Stern, take your clothes off."

Maybe the only way I was going to get it was through illusion: screens, veils. So I went to *Vogue* and said, "Can you get me some scarves? Scarves you can see through—with geometrics. And jewelry." Jewelry doesn't need too many clothes, right?

Vogue found a couple of dozen filmy scarves and some other odds and ends, and gave them to me. I threw it all in a bag and took it with me to California.

At the Hotel Bel-Air we were given an upstairs suite, Number 261. I saw immediately how I could turn the whole suite into a studio for Marilyn. There was a big living room and a smaller, adjoining bedroom with an archway in between. The bedroom would be her dressing room. There were two twin beds, and

25

I threw the colored scarves and costume jewelry on one. There was a dressing table with a mirror which she could use to make up, and there was a big bathroom in the back. From the dressing room it was just a few steps through the archway into the living room, which would become the studio.

Any room anywhere can be transformed into a studio. All you need is lights, enough space to set up the lights, and a simple background, like white or colored paper. I used to design setups to travel with, consisting of floods, strobes, and paper racks, so that I could recreate my studio wherever I was shooting. A studio is basically just a space. You shape and shade that space by how you light it. And that depends on whom you're going to photograph there and how you want the finished picture to look.

How did I want to photograph Marilyn Monroe?

I knew that I didn't want anything to limit her in time or space. I didn't want any sets or anything that would distract the eye from her or limit the depth of the background, like that red velvet in Kelley's calendar shot. I wanted pure Marilyn and I wanted her in space, a space made up of light . . . a clear nowhere. By covering the walls of the big living room/studio with white paper, I could create a field of light around Marilyn.

As my assistant and I hung yards of white no-seam on the walls, I thought about Picasso, spreading out fresh white paper to make a drawing. It would be one of those drawings in which a bearded man, or a man with a bull's head, is brooding over a woman's nude, sleeping figure, about to make love to her. The self-portrait of a horny artist. Like me. Except instead of horns I had a camera.

Lighting was important. There were some assignments where I could preconceive and preset the lights, but not with Marilyn. I'd seen her in person and I knew better than to try and guess what she was going to do or even how long she'd stay. Whatever happened between us through the camera would happen in its own moment and would be its own adventure. I'd have to be ready for anything.

That was the way I had photographed Gary Cooper. He walked into my studio, I took one look, and said to myself, that guy will never sit still for me. I'd better light the whole space, so wherever he goes, I can follow him. And I was right. He kept sitting down, standing up, walking around, twirling the Colt .45 I'd found for him as a prop. He was a fabulous character, restless and alive. Like Marilyn.

For her, I needed a lighting setup that would enable me to create any effect I needed, yet would free me to devote my time and energy to photographing Marilyn. That meant maximum flexibility with minimum time spent in moving equipment and making changes. In my studio, my assistants and I sometimes spent two or three hours resetting the lighting if I didn't like it. I knew if we took that kind of time with Marilyn, I'd lose her. She might wait around for a ten- or fifteen-minute change, but a two-hour change—never. Yet I wanted several possibilities at my fingertips. I

wanted the softness of backlight, but I also wanted to be able to add the clarity of front light, like direct sunlight. So I set up an umbrella, which I could turn on or off to create front light at the flick of a switch.

The mystery of Marilyn Monroe was challenging me to design a new, streamlined setup, one that would give me all the different lightings without moving anything but switches. I wanted all the plugs and wires and reflectors functioning as automatically as my eye and brain, so that photographing her would become almost as effortless as looking at her, and the click of the shutter could be the blink of an eye.

Besides creating a space of light, I wanted to create an environment of sound. I had brought my hi-fi, one turntable with speakers I could set up in different corners of the room. By '62 I had a portable system which I brought to every sitting, not just to lull the model, but because music made sense with posing in terms of movement. I had learned that from watching Allegra dance.

At that time I liked early rock and the Everly Brothers. The Beatles came just a year or two later, and then came the crazy successful days when I had a real juke box in my big studio, and I'd play a different song for each model, real quarters and all. But even in '62 no one played the music I was playing. I was the first juke-box photographer. It went right back to my beginnings at the soda fountain, where I used to make artistic ice-cream sodas in six colors, and wipe the counter and look at pretty girls, to the accompaniment of the juke box.

I looked around with satisfaction at my "studio." Lights, music, veils . . . what was missing?

The phone rang. It was Pat Newcomb, Marilyn's P.R. girl.

"Hi, Bert. Everything okay?"

"Fine."

"Would you order three bottles of 1953 Dom Perignon for Marilyn for tomorrow?"

"No problem," I said.

I went downstairs and jumped into my rented pink Thunderbird two-seater convertible. There was a place in L.A. that rented sports cars, and that was the only color they had that week. Pink. So I jumped in, drove down to a liquor store in Santa Monica, and asked if they had any '53 Dom Perignon.

They did.

"How many bottles would you like, sir?"

"I'll take a case," I said. It was eleven dollars a bottle then. It's fifty-five dollars a bottle now. But money was no object.

I loaded the case of champagne in the pink Thunderbird and drove back to the Bel-Air through the California twilight. The preparations for tomorrow were complete.

I was preparing for Marilyn's arrival like a lover, and yet I was here to take photographs. Not to take her in my arms, but to turn her into tones, and planes, and shapes, and ultimately into an image for the printed page.

Here I was, about to achieve every red-blooded American man's dream. I was going to get Marilyn Monroe, the real live girl, alone in a hotel room. And what was I going to do with her?

The truth was, I didn't know what was going to happen. Anything was possible. She might not show up at all. She might walk in and say, "Look, you've got twenty minutes," in which case I'd grab my lasting shot and leave. Or . . . she might say, "I've been waiting for you all my life. Let's run away together," in which case I would say, "Let's go," jump in the pink Thunderbird with her, drive off into the sunset, and never take another picture.

By now it was night, and there was nothing left to do but wait till tomorrow. Forget about sleep. After dark the Bel-Air turns on hidden Japanese stone lanterns in the garden, so I just walked around outside. It gets lonely there at night. To be there alone, missing Allegra, wanting Marilyn, was like wandering in a dream, down those outside corridors where there are swans, and flowers floating, into this little room in the middle of nowhere where the desk was, a very small room with very soft couches and beautiful rugs. The guy behind the desk had the ledger open.

"Oh yes, Mr. Stern! How are you tonight?" he said as I wandered through. No one else there, and he's got this big book in which he writes everything down . . . like the angel of God recording all your sins and transgressions. *Stern, Bert. Lust. Adultery. Gluttony!*

Wait a minute. What is all this guilt? I haven't done anything except set up some lights.

But you want to. You want to make love to Marilyn Monroe. You would if you could. You will if you can.

There were two Bert Sterns. One was the Bert Stern who had been accused of playing it close to the edge . . . who had married his first wife with his fingers crossed . . . who thought his second, real marriage was over six months after it began . . . who had an appointment with blond destiny. *That* Bert Stern would gamble everything he had for one night with Marilyn Monroe.

The other was Bert Stern, husband, father, provider, photographer, who was going to get the picture, get out of there, go home to his wife and baby, and live happily ever after.

I knew I should be a good boy and go for the pictures. Do the best I could with my camera. And if things got provocative, because I liked it hot, it would only make the pictures better.

It was a risk. And there are things that can make a man forget the best of intentions. Like Dom Perignon.

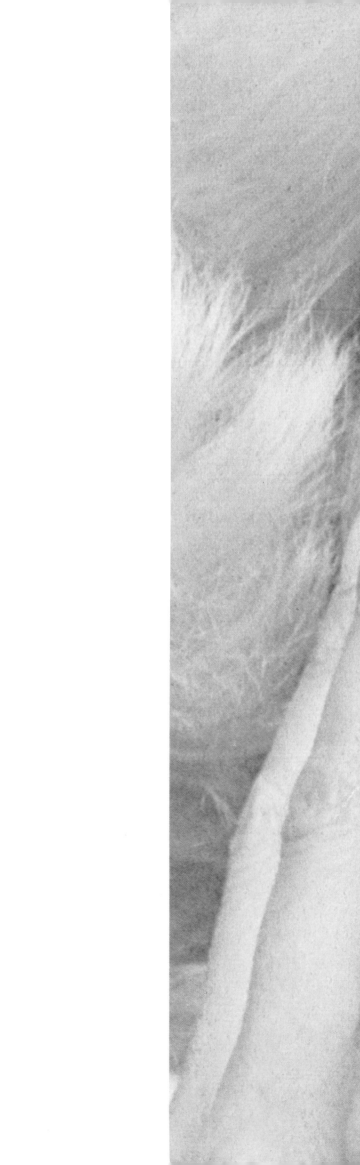

But as long as I kept a camera in my hands, I'd be safe.

She was supposed to come at two the next day. George Masters, the hairdresser she had chosen, arrived before two. He unpacked his combs and brushes and sprays while my assistant checked to make sure all the lights were ready and clicking. The night before I had had my moments of wondering what I needed all these people for, but now that I'd made up my mind to do this right, I wasn't sorry to have them around. Their help would free me to concentrate on Marilyn.

I was ready for her. The champagne was chilled, a record poised above the hi-fi turntable ready to drop, the scarves glowed on the bed. Everything seemed in a state of expectancy.

I waited.

Two o'clock came and went . . . three o'clock. Four. I'd heard that she was always late. It didn't bother me. I knew it took a long time to become Marilyn Monroe each day, and after all, it had taken me a whole lifetime to be sitting here waiting for her. That she was even coming was a great idea. I was prepared to wait until she got there, even if it was midnight, or the next day.

While I waited, I thought about all the Marilyns I had seen: turning and smiling in the spotlight of a party . . . cuddling up to Tony Curtis in *Some Like It Hot* . . . crying in the newsreels with dark glasses on . . . singing "Happy Birthday" to President Kennedy . . . screaming her heart out for the wild horses in *The Misfits.* I didn't know fact from fiction. To me she was just Marilyn, and she was beautiful in tears or in a fury. But if I had to point to one image and say, *"That's* Marilyn," it would be that moment in *The Misfits* when she's sitting across the breakfast table from Clark Gable. They've just spent the night together in the cabin, and she looks at him over a cup of coffee and says, "You really like me, don't you?"

I thought if I could just get *that* expression in my pictures, I'd have captured her.

But when five o'clock rolled around and there was still no Marilyn, both George and my assistant began to wonder whether she was going to show up at all. That was supposedly why they had fired her from *Something's Got to Give.* Hollywood was trying to whip her into shape, saying, "How many fans do you have? How many men are willing to leave their wives for you? Tough. You be at the studio at eight o'clock, or you're fired."

I thought they were idiots.

To me she was worth waiting for. If she did show up, I really didn't expect to have much time with her anyway. She'd probably walk in and say, "I only have an hour to shoot these pictures." Well, that would be enough. I was ready to settle for ten minutes—anything. To have her for even one picture would be worth it. But if she had time, I had nothing but time.

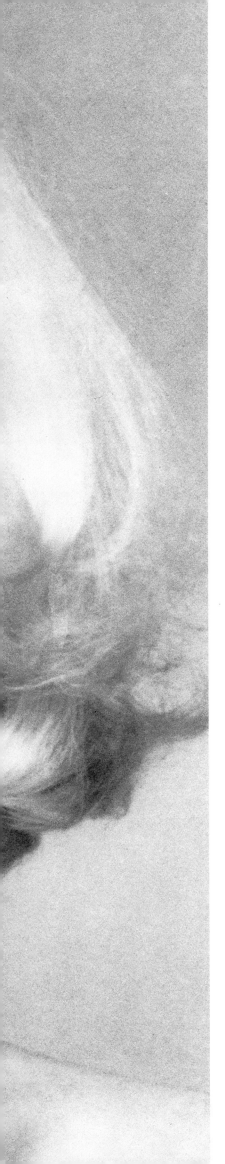

Now, though, I began to wonder. I thought, here I sit with all these high expectations, full of hope and wonder at the great romance I'm going to have, and there is no way, *no way* she can be as beautiful as my dream of her. In her movies and photographs, she's packaged in a very delicious way, with hairdressers and clothes and makeup. The fact is, she's well into her thirties, and she really was a little chubby when I saw her in *The Misfits.* I'd better be prepared, because when she comes, I'll have to deal with the real Marilyn Monroe.

The phone rang.

Startled out of my reverie, I grabbed it. The voice said, "Miss Monroe is here."

"She's here already?" I couldn't believe it. It was 7 P.M. She was only five hours late.

I slowly put the phone down and took a deep breath. *Well, Bert, this is it.* I wanted to see her first, before the others did, so I said, "Okay, everybody just stay right here. I'll be right back." And I stepped out the door.

As I came down the stairs toward the reception room, I was surprised to see a girl walking toward me on the pathway between the trellises, alone. A scarf covered her hair. I had expected her to be flanked by press agents and bodyguards and God knows who else. Her P.R. girl, Pat Newcomb, was supposed to be there for the sitting. But no. She had come alone.

The sun was setting behind the Hollywood hills, and the girl next door, the girl every man dreams of, was walking slowly toward me in the golden light. I walked up to her.

She was a total surprise.

This was no older woman, voluptuous, aging.

She had lost a lot of weight, and the loss had transformed her. She was *better* than the full-bodied, almost overblown girl I had seen in the movies. In her pale-green slacks and cashmere sweater she was slender and trim, with just enough softness in the right places—all of it hers. She had wrapped a scarf around her hair, and she wore no makeup. Nothing. And she was *gorgeous.*

I had expected—feared—an elaborate imitation. No. She was the real thing.

"Hi," I said, "I'm Bert Stern." I offered her my hand. She took it, and I looked into her eyes. They were blue, green-blue.

I forgot my marriage, my baby, my dream life in New York, everything but this moment.

I was in love.

I took a deep breath and said, "You're beautiful."

She looked straight at me, parted her lips, and said, "Really? What a nice thing to say." Another surprise: her voice. It wasn't the tiny, breathy baby voice you hear in her movies. It was more natural, yet distinctive and feminine. *She* was a natural. Not one of those Hollywood stars who were beyond my reach, but a real, flesh-and-blood girl named Marilyn. I had nothing to fear from her . . . except that she might vanish before my eyes now that I'd found her.

I had a camera to make sure that wouldn't happen.

"I've built you a studio," I told her as we walked up the stairs to the suite. I opened the door for her. She stepped across the threshold, said hello to George and Jim, and looked around at the white paper, the waiting lights. The familiar props of a photographic sitting seemed to set her at ease. She explored the room like a cat in a new house.

"Is there a dressing room?" she asked me.

I showed her the bedroom. She sat down in front of the vanity, took her scarf off, and shook out her hair. It was white blonde, almost silver. I looked at her in the mirror.

Her eyes met mine in the mirror. "What do you want to do?" she said.

"Are you in a hurry?" I said.

"No, why?"

"I thought you were going to have like five minutes."

She said, "Are you kidding?"

I said, "Well, how much time have you got?"

"All the time that we want!"

I looked at her, and I saw that it was true. She had nothing else to do. She wasn't going anywhere. She was *here*.

"That calls for some champagne," I said.

I popped open a bottle of Dom Perignon and poured two glasses. We drank.

Marilyn put her empty glass down on the vanity. I refilled it while she looked at herself in the mirror and began to take out her makeup.

I never really liked makeup on women. Of course it has a certain illusionary power. But if a girl was really gorgeous all made up, I always thought that if you took it all off, removed every trace of color from her face, she could be even *more* beautiful.

"How about doing it with no makeup?" I ventured.

She stared at me through the mirror. "No makeup?"

"Well, maybe just a little eyeliner," I said.

"And a little lipstick," she added.

"A little . . . very light. You don't need makeup."

She turned to look at me and laughed a little. "Oh, you want to be creative, huh?"

The moment she said those words to me, I knew that I could do no wrong with her. Because she was *really* creative. Open to anything, no matter how far out. Anything I could dream up, she'd probably be willing to do.

She took out a little bottle and started pouring some white, silky liquid onto her fingertips. "I always use Nivea," she said as she began to rub it into her skin.

I picked up my Nikon and watched her through the eyepiece. The 105-mm lens let me examine the intimate texture of her beauty, as if under a magnifying glass. Her skin was as fine and translucent as real silk. It had the faintest aura of golden down on it, like a peach. My eye roved her face, searching. I couldn't find the secret of her beauty in any one feature. She didn't have a great nose like Liz Taylor, or perfect lips like Brigitte Bardot. She didn't have gorgeous almond-shaped eyes like Sophia Loren. And yet she was more to me than all of them put together.

Sometimes when something is perfect in every detail, it's not beautiful anymore. It's impressive, it's even slightly intimidating, but you find yourself thinking, "Who could possess that?" Marilyn was *possessable.* Who cared if her lips weren't perfect? They were made for kissing.

As she leaned forward to apply her lipstick, her attention was caught by the bright colors of the scarves on the bed behind her. I saw her eyes go to them in the mirror, and then she put down her lipstick and turned around. She went over to the bed and touched the scarves curiously.

"What are these?" she said.

I didn't want to come right out and say it, so I said, "Oh . . . I don't know. Just some things I brought along to play with, if you like them."

She picked up the scarves one by one, looked at them, felt them, and then she held one up to the light. I could see her through the scarf. Her eyes turned blue.

She lowered the scarf, looked at me and said, "You want to do *nudes?*"

She'd seen right through it.

"Uh, well I—I guess so!" *Who, me?* "It'd probably be nice, wouldn't it? But it wouldn't be exactly nude. You'd have the scarf."

"Well, how much would you see through?"

"That depends on how I light it," I said.

"What do you mean?" she said. And then, "Just a second. George?"

George Masters came in. She said, "George, what do you think about these scarves and doing nudes?"

I held my breath.

"Oh . . . what a *divine* idea!" said George.

Thank God. If he had said, "Oh, no, how gauche," the whole thing would have been off in a second. Gone.

She was that vulnerable.

Then she said, "Well, what about my scar?"

"I didn't know you had a scar," I said. "What's that from?" How strange! Liz Taylor had had that scar on her throat, in Rome.

"I had my gallbladder removed six weeks ago," she said. "Will it show?"

"If it does, we can always retouch it," I said, to reassure her, although I hadn't retouched Liz Taylor's scar. To me a photograph is most powerful when it's least tampered with.

I remembered something Diana Vreeland had said to me. We were having lunch, and I told her I wanted to do a book on women. I thought she'd love the idea, but she said, "Darling, come back in twenty years, when you know a little bit more." And then she said, "I think there's nothing duller than a smooth, perfect-skinned woman. A woman is beautiful by her scars."

I didn't agree with her at the time. To my mind, a smooth, perfect-skinned woman was . . . perfect. But Vreeland's words had stayed in my mind. And here were these two great sex goddesses with their marks of mortality.

"I really don't think it will show too much behind the chiffon, with the designs and all," I said.

Marilyn hesitated.

"All right," she said.

Not more than fifteen minutes had passed since she'd arrived, and already she had agreed to take her clothes off! Suddenly the excitement was electric. What was I going to do now?

I got up. "I have to check the lights," I said, and I went into the studio. As I left the room, she was beginning to pull her sweater over her head.

It was great that she had agreed to pose with the scarves, but how the hell was I going to light it? I'd have to build up just the right balance of front light and backlight, so that some light came through the scarf to add translucency, and some came from the front to bring out the color of the scarf. It was tricky, delicate, and I wanted to make sure I didn't screw it up. I'd have to take a polaroid.

Before I had Polaroids for test shots, I would always think in the middle of taking pictures, "Boy, if these come out they're going to be great." But I never knew if they would or not, because I was not trained as a photographer. What little technical stuff I knew, I picked up when I was in the Army. Correct exposures remained somewhat mysterious to me.

Marilyn walked onto the set in her bare feet, a glass of champagne in one hand and an orange striped scarf tied around her bare bosom. She still had her green slacks on.

"I'm not going to take off my pants," she declared.

"Just roll them down, then," I said.

She rolled them way down low on her hips so I could see the label, which read "JAX."

I saw the scar now. It was on the right side of her stomach. A blemish, an imperfection that only made her seem more vulnerable and accentuated the incredible smoothness of her skin. She was the color of champagne, the color of alabaster . . . delicious all over. You could just dip your finger into her, like tasting a freshly made meringue. And yet she was insecure about how she looked. Before she'd even let me take a Polaroid, she called, "George!"

George came hurrying in.

Marilyn draped the scarf across her chest and said, "George, how does this look?"

"Oh, how wonderful! Oh, how beautiful!"

I snapped the Polaroid.

Okay, I had the lights almost exactly right. I wanted the feeling of light coming through the lens to lie on the film gently. Light as love. I wanted these pictures soft, but *sharp*. A sharp Marilyn floating in light.

I made one more Polaroid, trying to get rid of all the flare.

There, now I had it.

We were ready to begin.

I went over and started the record player: the Everly Brothers.

Marilyn frowned. "Don't you have any Frank Sinatra records?"

"No," I said. "Only Avedon plays that stuff."

Avedon had come into Brentano's one night when I was playing the Everly Brothers in one of those little booths with the earphones. I saw him walk in and I thought, I hope he doesn't see me, but of course he did. He opened the door and listened.

"Do you *like* that kind of music?" he said.

I said, "Yes."

And he said, "Boy," shaking his head. I could see the Frank Sinatra records under his arm.

I preferred the Everly Brothers.

"Dream,
Dream dream dream . . .
When I feel blue
In the night,
When I need you
To hold me tight,
Whenever I want you
All I have to do
Is dream . . ."

We drank champagne and concentrated on the pictures. It was hard, it really was hard, because she was *happening.* She was alive. A wild spirit, as fleeting as thought itself and as intense as the light that played on her. I couldn't freeze Marilyn and expect to get a picture from her. She was totally the opposite of Elizabeth Taylor. Liz Taylor's already *there.* All she has to do is turn exactly straight and be still. Her beauty is formal. Liz is the fact of beauty. Marilyn was the fantasy. If Marilyn were still for an instant, her beauty would evaporate. With her it was like photographing light itself.

She was much more of a partner than I'd expected. The first hour or two I had an idea of what I was after. I had all kinds of imagery floating

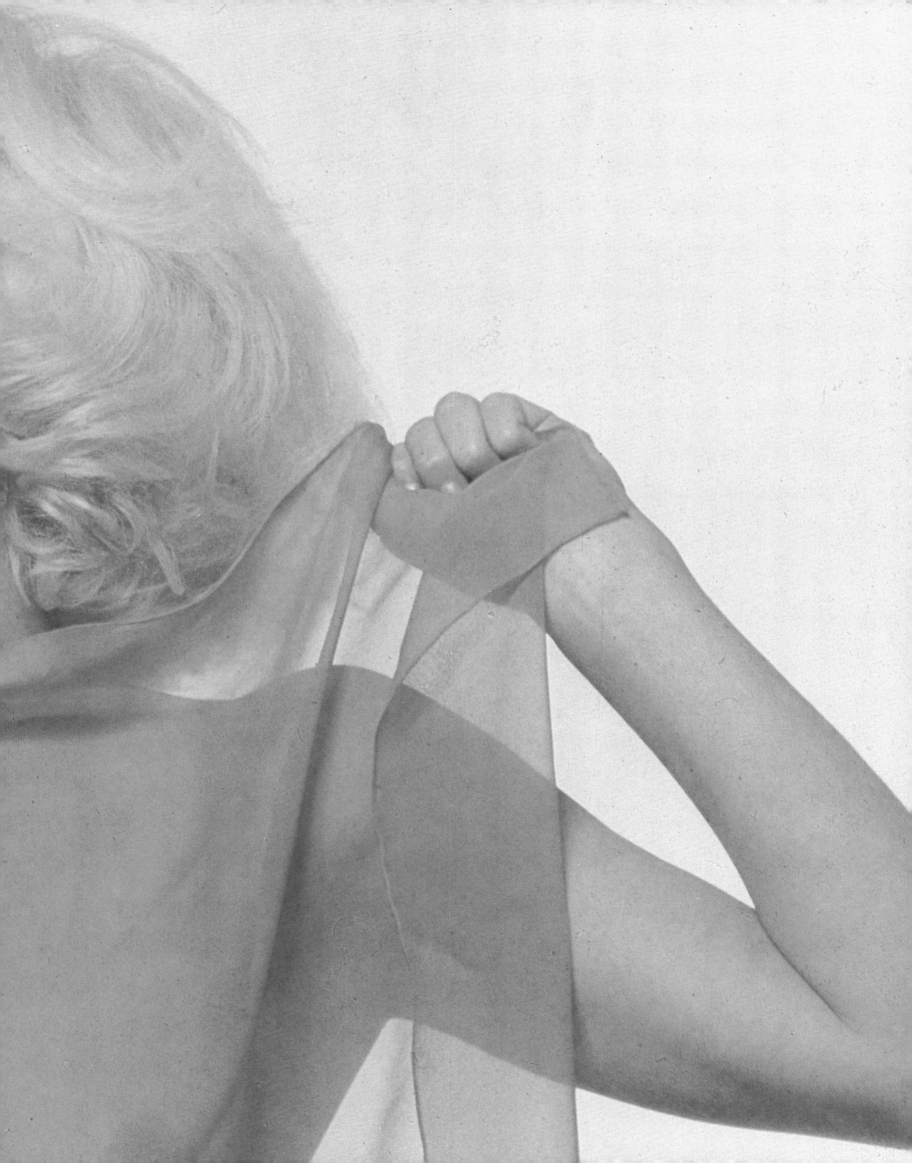

around, and she was picking up on it, performing it all. I didn't have to tell her what to do. We hardly talked to each other at all. We just worked it out. I'd photographed a lot of women, and Marilyn was the best. She'd move into an idea, I'd see it, quick lock it in, click it, and my strobes would go off like a lightning flash—PKCHEWW!!—and get it with a zillionth of a second.

At one point Marilyn was playing with a rose-colored scarf, and I caught her feeling herself up a little bit, feeling her own blossoming, her own . . . lusciousness. *What is this? Wow, what IS this?* I remembered when I was twelve, hiding in my parents' dark bedroom, spying on the pretty blond girl who lived across the street. Her name was Mary. She was about eleven years old, and she was just beginning to do things like that to herself, to run her hands over her new breasts and . . . *wow, what IS this?*

I didn't want her to see me, so I'd sit in the dark and look in the mirror, and through the mirror I could see out the window across to her window—like looking through the camera at Marilyn. I sat there for an hour once, waiting, wondering, hoping that she'd play with herself while I was watching. And sure enough, her hand stole under that pink sweater.

The next morning she saw me on the street and said, "If you don't stop looking at me, I'm going to tell your mother!"

I was just as curious about women, just as awed and mystified now as I was when I was twelve. But I had been given a magic machine that made it all right. The camera was the magic that transported me to the dream: Marilyn, Mary, the blonde, the girl next door, right here in my hotel room with almost no clothes on.

Her innocence amazed me. Here was a girl you'd think would be super aware of guys coming on to her, and she just went right *past* that, into another space that was far more childlike and interesting. I think there's a child in all of us, which may be the part that's most real, but for most of us it's very hard to free. Not with Marilyn. She was real, like a little child. Real in her sexuality and just as real in her modesty.

Every time she tried a new scarf, or a more daring pose, she'd call out "George!"

George Masters would come running in, and she'd say doubtfully, "What do you think?" George would reassure her.

Finally we got down to the two chiffon roses. I handed them to her, and all she could do was hold them in front of her, one over each breast.

Now she was really getting turned on. I could see it, I could feel it. And if I didn't shoot when she expected me to, she'd laugh. All I had to do was pause for two seconds, miss a beat, or change my mind and do something off tempo, and she'd respond. And we would go a step higher.

By now I'd already reached the point of my expectation. The only place to go was beyond, into something even I didn't know about. Usually that's hard, to exceed myself. A lot depends on the mood and the model. With some people it's one . . . two . . . three . . . so I may just work up

to that point where I've got what I was after, and stop. But every once in a while someone walks into my life who's super alive. And because she's super alive, I get to experience my own super aliveness. Marilyn and I just jumped from one to seven and went right into eight. And we entered into another space, in which no one existed but us.

Somewhere in the middle of the night, outside of time, it happened. We began to open up whole new phases and dimensions, to go into pictures that were closer to the truth and harder to capture, pictures I knew I'd like even more when I saw them. I could feel those pictures when they happened, and so could she. They made her laugh and me smile. We weren't just making love, we were making pictures.

There's no greater sensation than making love with a camera. *Right for me is right for you . . . can't you feel it when you're on and see it when it misses?* The music was playing, the strobes were clicking—kchk-kchk-kchk-kchk-kchk—when they really get going they talk to you, those lights. They make you laugh, because they click with your mind, and you really know it's *you* that is clicking. And she's clicking. So the whole room's clicking, flickering like heat lightning, and the lights go *blam* and the room goes dark and the light exists only when I shoot the picture. . . . I look at her, she has blue eyes, green eyes . . . and all of a sudden it's quiet. The music's quiet. We're out in space. We're out of this world. I'm out here in the absolute, taking photographs.

When you take pictures that way, you're in another mental state. You don't have to ask questions. Your brain is on automatic. That automatic system knows all the f-stops, knows everything. All you have to do is just think of anything you want, anything, and you can have a picture of it. And those are the ones that really knock you out when you look at them. They're so simple. So far out. They have a greater life.

Marilyn had the power. She was the wind, that comet shape that Blake draws blowing around a sacred figure. She was the light, and the goddess, and the moon. The space and the dream, the mystery and the danger. But everything else all together, too, including Hollywood, and the girl next door that every guy wants to marry.

I thought she would make a great wife. I could have hung up the camera, run off with her, lived happily ever after, and never taken another picture. But we had come there for the photographs.

And that's finally what it was. Two people getting off on taking photographs. For ourselves, but not just for ourselves. The world was watching. We had Kodak to develop our shenanigans, *Vogue* to print them, and people all over the world to see the pictures.

It was late, close to dawn, when I finally got all her clothes off. I handed her a black-and-white scarf with a bold pattern of alternating stripes. You could see through the pale stripes, but the dark stripes veiled and masked parts of her. I was fascinated by the juxtaposition of black and white, Marilyn in light and shadow, so I stopped and switched to black-

and-white film. As I looked through the viewfinder, I realized that the scarf should hang almost straight down to display the pattern. That way it would reach from her shoulders to her knees. For this one I needed her bare legs—Marilyn from head to toe.

"You know, for this one you've really got to take your pants off," I said.

I expected her to call for George, who by now was falling asleep in the other room. But she just said, "Okay." We'd already gone so far in the pictures; what was there to be shy about? She stepped into the shadowy archway between the rooms and, holding the scarf around her like a towel, wriggled out of her slacks. And then she walked back out onto the white paper.

I started to shoot. This was the way I'd wanted her all along. Her beautiful body shone through the harlequin scarf in a tantalizing, abstract hide-and-seek.

Until she dropped it. And I shot it. Just for myself.

One glimpse, one stolen frame.

We were finished.

It was almost seven in the morning. We'd been working for twelve hours. While she got dressed, I piled up all the rolls of film. Then she said a quiet good-bye and left. I just stood there like a dazed lover.

It had been a once-in-a-lifetime experience. Absolutely once in a lifetime. I got what I really wanted.

I had all those beautiful pictures and I was still pure.

My love affair with Marilyn was over.

As soon as I got back to New York, I sent the color film to the lab. The few rolls of black-and-white I began developing myself, slowly, very carefully, testing, and I made contact sheets. It took five days before I got all the color back. I went over them and marked the ones I liked best with my initials in red grease pencil. Then I gathered everything together in one big envelope and took it up to show Alex Liberman at *Vogue*.

In 1962 things had changed for Alex, too. He had just been promoted from chief art director of all the Condé Nast magazines to the even more powerful position of editorial director. His new office was on the eighteenth floor of the Graybar Building at 420 Lexington Avenue, one floor below the art department where I had first met him some years before. As I got out of the elevator I remembered the awe I had felt approaching Alex's office that first day. I wanted to be a *Vogue* photographer, and here was the man who had made *Vogue* one of the most powerful showcases for photographers in the world. In 1962 he *was Vogue*. He still is.

Alex's new office was all white, completely different from the black paneled office he'd had before. I paused for a moment in the doorway just to look at him. He was impeccably dressed, as always: tan summer suit, blue shirt, knit tie. His hair was black with streaks of gray at the temples, and he had a small European moustache.

I tapped on the doorframe.

Alex looked up and said, "Oh, dear boy, come in!"

I handed him the thick envelope. He took it over to the long light box that lined one wall of the office, and together we spread out the photographs of Marilyn.

Alex picked up his magnifying glass and bent over the pictures. I could see that he was really looking at them.

I held my breath.

"*Marvelous,*" he said.

Now *Vogue* never says anything negative. Even if they're not going to use something, it's divine. But Alex really seemed to love them. "They're lovely, Bert," he said. "Fabulous."

I felt he was going to use one. I also knew enough to keep my mouth shut about *which* one. Past experience had taught me that if I said, "I like *that* one," he might disregard it. It was better if he chose them anyway. Alex's taste was unerring. He had picked my first, and probably my best, *Vogue* cover, and I knew I could count on him to find the most interesting pictures of Marilyn.

Alex sat back. "We'll see, we'll see. They're marvelous, really wonderful. I must look at them more carefully. Leave them with me, let me show them to Miss Daves, and Mrs. Vreeland"—Diana Vreeland was just in the process of taking over from Jessica Daves as editor-in-chief of *Vogue.*

So I went back to my East Thirty-ninth Street studio happy, with visions of a color double-spread of Marilyn Monroe nude in *Vogue.* I opened the door, and before I even had a chance to ask what was going on, Vickie said, "*Vogue* called."

I said, "Already?"

Oh, boy.

I went up the stairs to my office, and called *Vogue.* Alex came right on the phone.

"Bert, we just *love* the pictures," he said. "But"—here it comes, I thought—"they're so beautiful, they're so wonderful, they're so gorgeous, we want you to do more."

"*More?*" I said.

They didn't have enough pictures?

He said, "Yes, we love the pictures so much that we'd like to give it eight pages. But we need more black-and-white. Would you be willing to do more if we can arrange it?"

My mind was working fast. Eight pages. Black-and-white. That meant

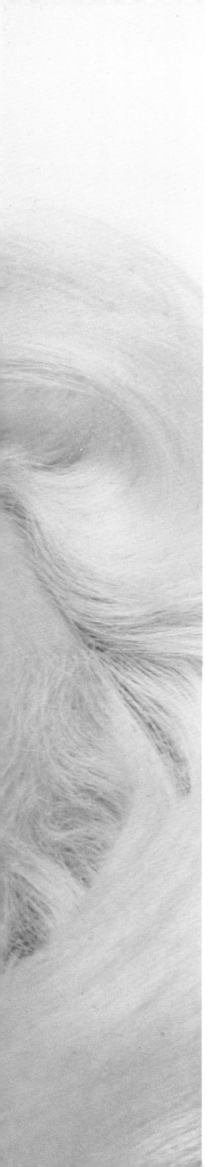

fashion pages. And that meant that they didn't want to run just nudes. They were probably going to get a lot of clothes, cover her up.

Actually I would have been happy with one page, one nude of Marilyn. I'd been trained that way. In advertising you go for that one great shot, the one that's going to step out of the book and *stop* you: "Hi, my name's Marilyn! What's yours?" I had shot the nudes with the size and shape of the *Vogue* page in mind. I'd already seen my Liz Taylor picture and it was full-page. To run one full-page Marilyn would have been just fine with me.

But what the hell. If they wanted to run eight pages of her, I wasn't going to complain about shooting fashion. And black and white . . . come to think of it, I'd never shot that one great black and white I wanted, had I? I'd gotten so involved with the scarves and all, I completely forgot the picture I had come for.

Not to mention the romance I had had in mind.

I'd thought I was all finished with Marilyn, but it seemed that fate was taking a hand.

"You want me to go *back* to California?"

"Yes, Yes," said Alex, "if she'll pose again. By all means, by all means."

"Fine with me," I said. "If Marilyn will pose, I'll go back."

"Wonderful. We'll call her."

The next day *Vogue* called again. Marilyn had said yes. She liked shooting at the Bel-Air, so I was to call them again and make arrangements—for *three* days and nights this time. And there was more. "We're having Kenneth flown out especially for the sitting," Alex said. "And we want the best, the very best editor to go with you. We're sending Babs Simpson."

This thing was getting bigger and bigger. Kenneth was the best and most successful hairdresser in America. If you could choose anyone in the whole world to do Marilyn Monroe's hair, who would you want but Kenneth?

The fact that *Vogue* was sending an editor on the shoot was a sign that they were getting serious. The first time they'd let me go off and do whatever I wanted, but now they had realized that I was on to something, and they were going to make sure they got what *they* wanted. Babs Simpson and I had worked together many times, and she understood me. I was sure they'd chosen her as the editor who could let me be the most creative and at the same time keep the most control. "Keep her clothes on," they'd probably told Babs. They saw where *I* was heading.

An editor has the difficult job of picking out all the fashions for a sitting, dressing the girl so that she looks just right, and helping the photographer in the best way possible. Babs Simpson was great because she knew when to step in and help, but she also knew how to leave the photographer alone with the model. I thought of her as "the needlepoint editor," because at every sitting, while the girl was doing her makeup or the photographer was shooting, Babs would sit on the side and work on needlepoint. Her whole house is decorated with pillows, rugs, the most beautiful things you've ever seen, which she made just sitting around studios over the years while the lights flashed.

As soon as I got off the phone with *Vogue*, I called up the Bel-Air.

This time I asked for a bigger space, the biggest suite they had. Mr. Landon, the assistant manager, said, "Oh, yes. That would be the bungalow, Number Ninety-six. It's a cottage of three rooms, separate from the rest of the hotel. Will that do?"

"It sounds perfect," I said, and I booked it for three nights. More space, more time with her . . . and more people.

This new arrangement meant I'd probably have to abandon my fantasy of getting her alone with all of her clothes off. Or would it?

Well . . . it was still possible. We'd had a great working rapport last time. Maybe this time she'd take it a step further and invite me over to her house. And if she looked at *me* across the table and said, "You really like me, don't you," was there any question what my answer would be?

Dream on, Bert Stern.

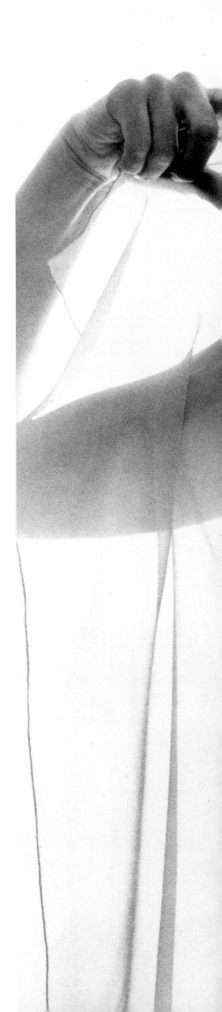

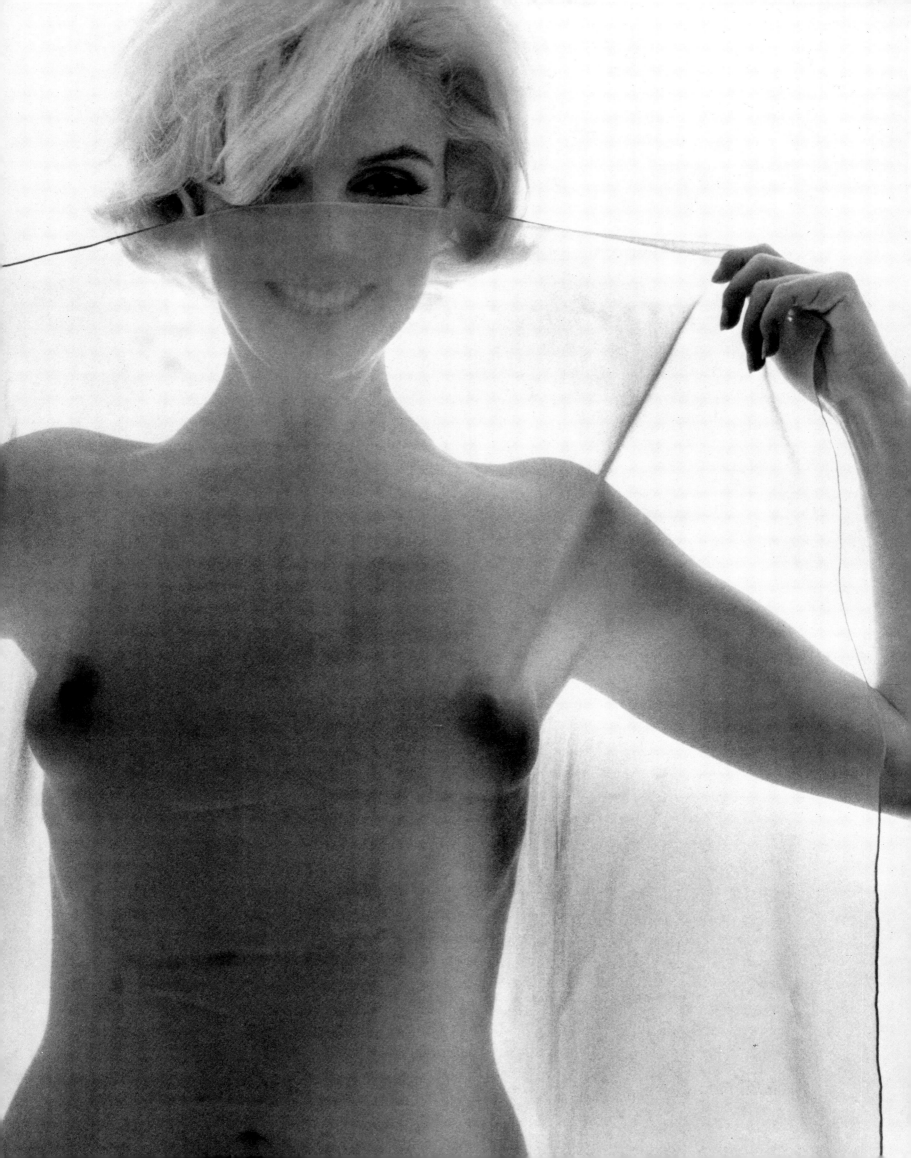

Babs was bringing all the clothes, so I flew out to California with my assistant, Peter Deal, and we started setting up in the bungalow of the Bel-Air.

It was a little pink house, off by itself on the grounds of the hotel, very private. There was a small sitting room, a kitchen, and a giant bedroom, with a high ceiling and sloping rafters. This time I decided to shoot the pictures in the bedroom.

We cleared out most of the furniture, except for a daybed, and I set up the strobes and paper racks and, of course, my portable sound system. Babs arrived from the airport in a limousine. When I saw the heaps of designer dresses and fur coats being carried into the bungalow, I had to laugh.

Vogue was certainly going in the opposite direction from my original idea. "We're going to get wonderful, wonderful clothes for her," they'd told me. "All the beautiful things you've ever dreamed of. We're going to make her into a princess!" And I'd thought, she's already a goddess. What does she need to be a princess for?

Well, at least we had plenty of Dom Perignon. Not only that, we were having a case of Château Lafite-Rothschild brought in—nothing but the best. For the Best. I also had a little pink heart-shaped pill in my pocket. It was a Dexedrine—not that I knew what that was then. Our family doctor had given me a bottle of them. "If you get tired in the afternoon, take a half of one of these," he'd said. In 1962 I didn't know much about drugs. The sixties were just beginning, and I was innocent. Not only had I never smoked marijuana, I'd never even heard of it. I'd never swallowed anything more dangerous than champagne. Women were drug enough for me.

Later that morning Kenneth arrived. Babs had all the clothes organized and ready and she worked seriously on her needlepoint while we sat in the garden waiting for Marilyn. *Vogue* had set up the sitting again for two o'clock, figuring that would give us plenty of time. I just laughed to myself. Last time it was set for two, and I felt lucky when she showed up at seven. But when four o'clock came, Babs folded up her needlepoint, put it in her bag, and said, "if she isn't here in an hour, I'm leaving."

It was the same attitude Marilyn had had to struggle against all her life. It was an attitude I never understood. Goddesses don't play by the rules. Now *Vogue* was refusing to make her special. Never mind how much of herself Marilyn was giving to us. She would either toe the line, play by the rules, or forget it. They didn't seem to understand that it took a long time to transform Norma Jean Baker into Marilyn Monroe.

Well, there was no point in my getting upset. I already had the photographs I wanted. *Vogue* could use those, and I wouldn't have to work so hard with the fashion. But I said, "Look, just give her till five. We're all staying here in the hotel anyway, so what's the difference?"

Babs agreed to wait. That crisis had been averted, at least for the moment. But not half an hour later my assistant, Peter, came over to me looking pale. In his polite way he said, "Bert, I really regret having to tell you this."

Oh my God, I thought. Something's broken.

"I am feeling quite sick to my stomach," he said.

At that moment Marilyn walked in.

If I had come with an entourage this time, so had she. She was flanked by Pat Newcomb and a big husky guy who looked like a bodyguard. I found out later that his name was Joe, and he was supposed to do her eyeliner. Marilyn saw Peter standing there all crumpled over and she walked right up to us. I was momentarily startled. I hadn't seen her in two weeks.

"What's the matter?" she asked, like she was part of the team. "Is he sick?"

"Never mind me," Peter said, wincing.

"You just sit right down," she ordered him. "I have a wonderful doctor, and I'm going to call him. Where's the phone?"

And then suddenly Peter was well. It was as if her concern had healed him. I was willing to attribute just about anything to her. That she was capable of performing magic I didn't question. He had probably been suffering from nervousness more than anything, since so much rested on his getting everything set up exactly right. I was glad the emergency was over. It had taken the edge off and made us a team again. And now that Marilyn was here, Babs cheered up, too, and went right to work. The whole crew was there, and we were in business.

I looked around at all these *people*, busy getting Marilyn dressed, applying her makeup, doing her hair, pouring champagne, adjusting the lights—all the process and anxiety that accompanies high fashion Voodoo. I realized that I was not going to have a love affair with Marilyn Monroe this time, either. This time I was going to do exactly what I'd been sent to do: take fashion pictures for *Vogue.* And I *needed* all those people, because this was going to be one tough assignment.

It was time to buckle down and start shooting all those clothes.

There she was, beautifully dressed, groomed, and perfect, standing in a gorgeous gown, wearing six-hundred-dollar shoes, diamonds and furs— the works. I had bright lights shining on her so I could focus. I was in the dark. She said, "What do you want me to do?"

I said, "Well . . . I guess maybe you shouldn't chew gum."

She took out the gum and handed it to me. I stuck it on the camera.

"Now," I said, "all I want you to do is sit there. Just sit down."

"Just sit here?"

"Just sit there while I get the lighting set up." It wasn't right. She looked so great, but if I got flare or something on that picture— "I have to do a Polaroid," I said.

While I was setting up the test shot, she asked shyly, "How are the

pictures from last time? I'd love to see them."

I said, "They're beautiful. *Vogue* loves them.

"Then why are we doing more?"

"They want you in fashion," I shrugged. I snapped the Polaroid. It was good.

So we went on: sipping champagne, taking pictures, struggling for some spontaneity in those formal clothes. But Marilyn was so beautiful, she brought her own romance to whatever she put on. The way she looked with her hair done, all delicious and made up, made you want to take her out and buy her a candlelight dinner with a single rose on the table and the best champagne in the house. And *then* take her home and slowly remove every stitch of clothing, like unwrapping the best, most expensive present in the world.

Vogue wanted to dress Marilyn up in beautiful clothes and I still thought the right thing to do was take her clothes off. The more they added, the more I tried to think of ways to reveal her. All she had to do was show one toe and it got *me* excited, so I took pictures like that.

The chinchilla was great. A floor-length chinchilla coat—what could be more of a cover-up than that? How could I get around it? I asked her to drape it on backward and let one leg peek out. *She* was willing. She didn't rebel against what *Vogue* wanted, because she saw the value of it, but she jumped at the chance to do something a little bit playful and provocative. Watching her image in the ground glass, I saw her right hand touch her hair behind her head as if she wanted to let her hair down. "Don't move," I said. "Just stay as you are and stick a little more of your left knee out of the coat." She didn't move her hand and slowly a naked knee appeared from beneath the ten-thousand-dollar fur coat.

There was always a little disagreement about the accessories Babs had brought. I didn't see the point to most of them. The white veil was almost strange enough to be interesting but that black wig . . . what was *that* all about? The last way I would have imagined Marilyn Monroe was as a raven-haired brunette. I guess nobody saw her that way, because I'd heard that she wore a black wig when she didn't want to be recognized. The very black hair with her white skin and red lips made her look like Snow White about to accept the poisoned apple from the witch.

On the other hand, Babs didn't want me to take pictures with the hat, and I thought the hat looked beautiful on her.

"It's just not good fashion, Bert," Babs said with editorial finality.

I felt compelled. Something was pushing me to take that picture. And that impulse went back to my original conception. I was after one picture to compare to Steichen's Garbo and there was something Garbo about that hat. I'd always thought Marilyn was unconsciously creating herself out of the great stars before her—Jean Harlow, Lana Turner, Betty Grable. She was all the blondes in all the movies she'd ever seen. When I saw her in "*Some Like It Hot*" I realized she must have seen herself in

Ginger Rogers too. Who would have thought there was a little of Garbo hiding inside Marilyn Monroe? I was seeing other aspects of Marilyn emerge . . . parts she had kept hidden and only now was sharing with herself and the camera. Shy elegance and dignity was now coming to the surface: It was an unknown Marilyn and it would demand a whole new kind of role for her.

Babs had brought a lot of black dresses—the hardest thing in the world to shoot. I supposed it was part of *Vogue's* black-and-white obsession, their answer to my color pictures. All I really needed was one good frame of each fashion, and if I shot enough, I'd be bound to get it. She was trying and I was trying, and certainly I was getting something. I was too high to be failing. High on the song of the strobes and high on champagne. Champagne did not impair my vision. I've always felt my vision was clear enough to cut through almost anything . . . in fact the higher I got the clearer things became. The truth was in front of me, and every time I flashed the light I saw her coming at me.

You try to photograph the truth . . . you frame it . . . you outline it using nothing but white light. Then you press the button. And if you're in tune, on that rare wavelength, you'll get to see the truth in black and white and circle it with red grease pencil.

Marilyn put on the simplest black dress. Kenneth combed her hair back. She sat on a chair. She was beautiful. All I had to do now was backlight it. That image was of the essence of black and white . . . and blonde. In a sense working for *Vogue* is very pure. *Vogue* is the ultimate in the world of fashion. You try to make something worthy of that, something classic.

The only thing I regretted with all this black and white was that I didn't have daylight. Daylight is unique because it's natural. Like Marilyn. The real thing usually possesses subtleties that simply can't be recreated artificially. A beautiful daylight portrait has more texture to it—it has an intensity that holds your attention just a little longer than one lit with a strobe. If I could have Marilyn in my daylight studio, the pictures would be even better. But we were working in a dark room, and the sun had long since dropped away behind the California hills. And I had come a long way from the days when I refused to use anything but daylight.

I knew how to come as close as possible to the quality of daylight using strobe lights. Strobe had the advantage of being able to stop action faster. With Marilyn I wanted to shoot fast. Even standing still her expressions were so fleeting, her moods so mercurial, I never knew how long she'd hold still for me to click that shutter.

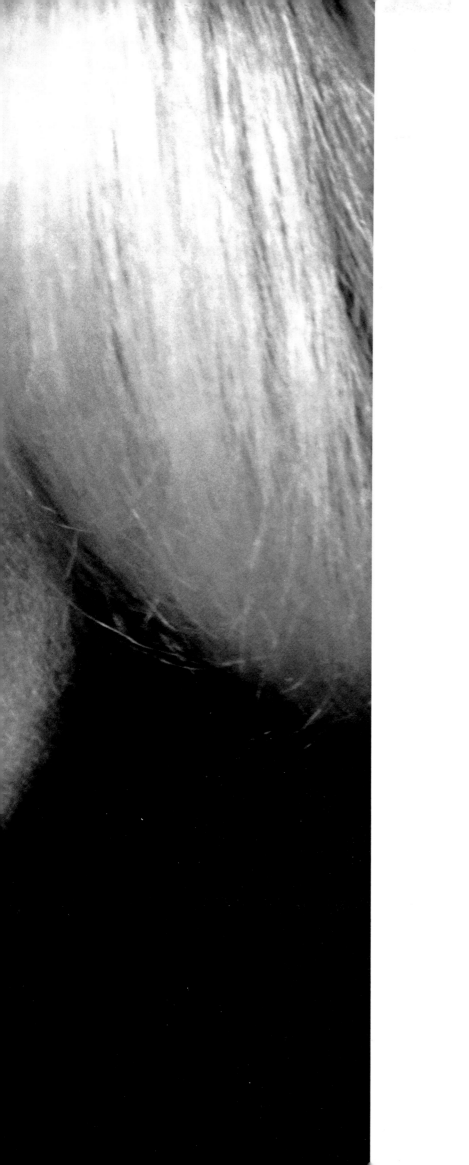

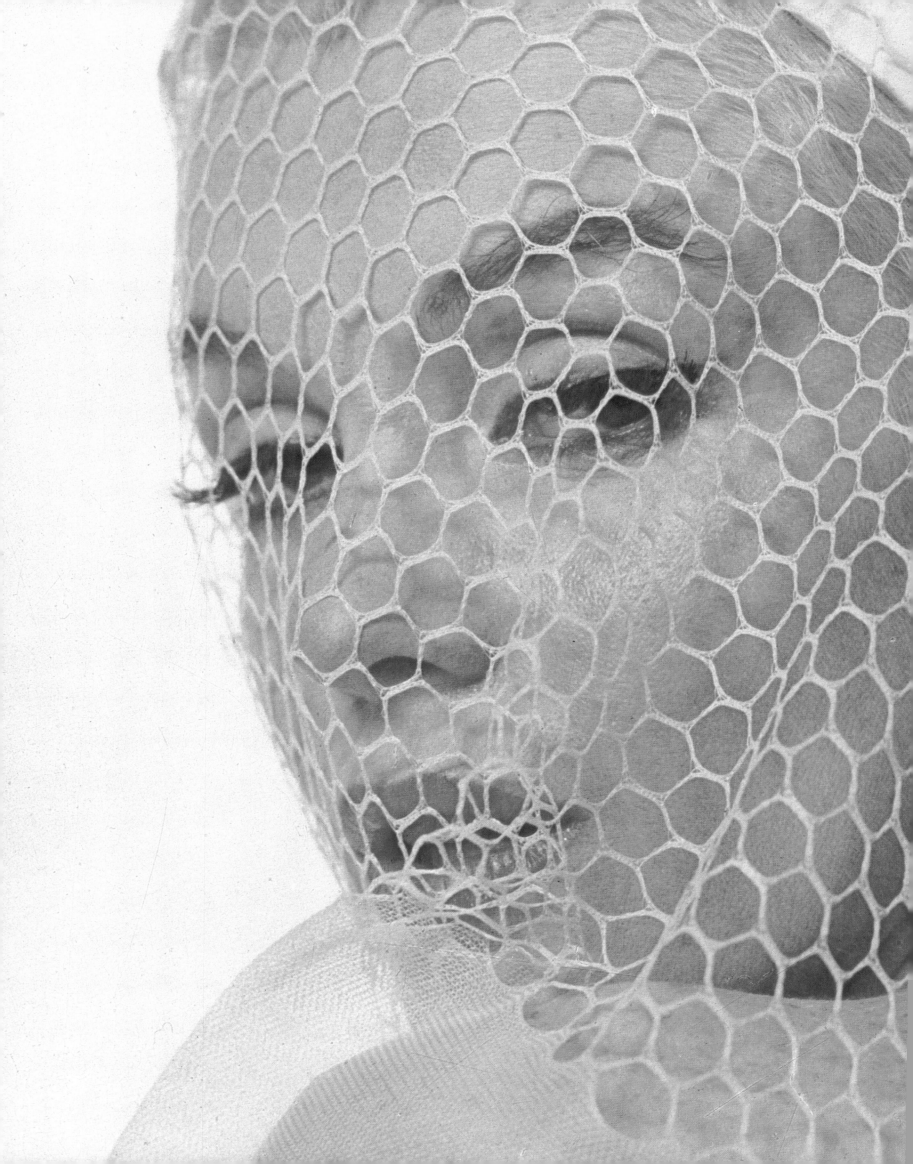

She was beginning to lose patience. I could see it on her face. She had been a good sport, but it was well after midnight, and the fashion was wearing thin. Besides, if I was drunk by now she was far from sober herself. I'd been sticking to Dom Perignon, but around the middle of the sitting I noticed that someone was spiking hers with 100 percent vodka. That was a guaranteed way to get her very bombed. It could also create a very volatile situation.

One thing I knew for sure—it wouldn't be any fun to get in Marilyn's way if that combustible mixture ever ignited—and I could feel the storm clouds gathering.

I got down on my knees in front of her to shoot a low angle shot. Suddenly she seemed so cold . . . I had the crazy idea that maybe she'd take pity on me if I knelt down to pay proper respect to her as the greatest symbol of woman that America had ever created. What I envisioned was an image of Marilyn that would be symbolic and sexy. I saw her in the nude wrapped in a chiffon American flag. That would make a great picture. Unfortunately there were no chiffon stars and stripes around. Instead, there stood Marilyn in a black dress, looking down at me. Getting madder.

"Why don't you direct a movie?" she said out of the blue.

"Uh-huh," I said, without lowering the camera from my eye. Direct a movie? I was having enough problems getting a few great photographs.

She picked up her champagne glass, took another sip and said, "What's your premise?"

My premise? What a strange question. I didn't know what my premise was. I didn't know a photograph needed one. I didn't know how to answer, so I flashed off a few more frames on my knees to distract her. Usually when I am looking up at a woman, she seems more beautiful. It's sexier in a way. But Marilyn wasn't yielding.

I could feel her slipping away through my fingers. Admittedly we'd been working for hours. I'd done all these fashion shots for *Vogue,* and they were beautiful, but what did I really have of Marilyn? Of course, I hadn't come here to get *her* . . . but that *was* what I really wanted, wasn't it?

But more, even more than that, I wanted something no one else could get from Marilyn, captured in a photograph forever.

That was my premise. I was down on my knees to her and I wanted her to award me herself. To knight me by giving herself. And she was saying, *You're too talented to be given something so easily.* Not in words, but by the way she stood there looking at me, by the challenge in her eyes.

Marilyn and I had unfinished business, it seemed. I wanted something more from the pictures, and she wanted more from me as a person. I could sense it.

But what?

I got to my feet. "I think we've done enough of this dress," I said. "Lets take a break."

Why was I so tired? The first time we'd worked all night without fatigue. Of course, then we'd been doing what we wanted. We hadn't had the whole Establishment to please.

As I went to get a glass of champagne, I remembered the little heart-shaped pill in my pocket. The doctor had said, "If you get tired in the afternoon, take half." I was certainly tired. And there was no way I was going to stop until I got what I wanted. Maybe that little pill would help keep me going.

I took it out of my pocket. The little pink heart complemented the yellow of the champagne and the green of the bottle. I broke it in two, put half in my mouth, took a sip of Dom Perignon, and swallowed.

All the craziness of the sixties really began for me at that moment. But I didn't know that. All I knew was that after a few minutes a kind of cold energy flowed into my bloodstream. It wasn't much, just enough to bounce me around a few times and put a nice sharp edge on my fatigue.

Babs had dug up yet another black dress, and I was ready for anything. But Marilyn had had it.

"Do we have to do any more of this fashion?"

"We're really almost finished, " I said. "Just one or two more dresses."

"I'm tired of all these clothes," she said. "Isn't there anything else to shoot around here?"

She looked around and then she walked off the white no-seam and grabbed a flimsy bed jacket that was lying casually on a chair near the strobe. I had tossed it there as a "no" when we were going through the clothes earlier, because Babs said it was bad fashion, and I didn't think much of it either. But Marilyn zeroed right in on it.

"Well, what about this?" she demanded, holding it up. It was a double layer of frills over black chiffon. "Is this fashion?"

"Well, I didn't think it was that nice," I started to say. But her mind was made up.

"I think it's *very* nice," she said, and she stormed off into the bathroom to change.

I looked at Babs. Babs looked at me. I shrugged, as if to say, it's not my fault. *I* didn't tell her to put it on.

"Bert, this is a waste of time," Babs said. "We can't run a picture of that. It's terrible. Tacky."

I said, "I know, but what am I going to do? It's late, and she's really been working hard. I'd better do a few pictures of her in the bed jacket."

The bathroom door opened, and Marilyn came out in this *thing*. Two layers of chiffon, a towel around her bottom, and that's all.

Babs winced. Kenneth threw up his hands.

Marilyn ignored them.

She came right up to me and lifted one layer of lace. I could see right

through the sheer black chiffon . . . those beautiful breasts.

And she said, "How's this for thirty-six?"

She didn't mean her bust size. She meant her age.

I looked her straight in the eye, "I'm not afraid of you, Marilyn."

I turned to Babs. "Why doesn't everybody just leave the room and let me shoot her alone?"

Babs said, "I think that's a good idea, Bert." Everyone got up and began to file out of the room. As they were leaving Babs said, "We'll be right out here if you need us."

"Great," I said, and I closed the door and locked it.

I turned around. Marilyn Monroe stood in the center of the room, backlit, with nothing on but a towel and a little bit of chiffon. Waiting.

We were alone. There was no one to tell us to shoot another dress or straighten another hair. This was just for us. Our scene . . . the brash photographer from Brooklyn and the sexiest woman in the world.

"What do you want to do?" she said.

What did I want to do? I didn't know where to begin. Looking around the room for a starting point, my eyes went straight to the daybed in the corner. I walked over to it, scooped up the lenses and boxes of film strewn on the bedspread, and pulled off the spread and blanket, leaving just the white sheets. Still cradling my Rolleiflex in one hand, with the strobe cord dangling, I dragged the bed to the middle of the room where the lighting was focused. Marilyn was watching.

"Here," I said. "Why not just get in the bed?"

Marilyn lay down between the bedsheets.

"Why don't you take the towel off?" I suggested. "It'll make bumps."

She reached down under the sheet, and then she raised her arm up high and handed me the towel. I took it and put it on the other side of the room. As I turned back, I caught a glimpse of her in the mirror we had used during the fashion shooting to show her what she looked like. I put on some music, picked up the bottle of Dom Perignon, walked backward toward her, watching her in the mirror, and sat down on the edge of the bed. Now I saw myself sitting beside her in the mirror. It was like a dream. In front of the mirror were her shoes, an empty bottle of Château Lafite-Rothschild, a cable release, and some used film boxes.

I picked up my Nikon and shot a picture of me and her.

She was really on, rolling around on the bed and giggling. I sat there trying to figure out the exposure without taking a Polaroid. I didn't want to do anything to turn her off. Because whatever else this was, it was one hell of a photographic opportunity. Here she was, ready to be something I'd never seen in the movies or anywhere. Right before my eyes, she was turning into an animal made of light. There was no time to stop. I set the camera at f/8.

I took a few shots, with the bed jacket falling down, and then I

stopped. It wasn't right. I was taking bad pictures; I could feel it. Momentarily I was at a loss. But when I'm taking pictures, I trust my intuition. If something's wrong, all I have to do is *stop*. I simply stand there, and after a few moments what I have to do will come to me. It didn't take long to figure it out.

"You know," I said, "you're beautiful. But that bed jacket is . . . it's not . . . well, frankly, it's terrible. What are we going to do with it?"

"I'll take it off!"

"Why don't you do that?"

"But what should I wear?"

"You could just wrap yourself in the sheet," I suggested.

"Oh! Okay." And she wriggled out of the bed jacket under the sheet, while I kept on shooting.

The bed jacket slipped to the floor.

There was nothing but a sheet between me and the fire.

What was I going to do now?

"Just a second," I said to Marilyn. I went to the door and opened it. "Kenneth, could you come in here for a minute?"

"Sure, Bert," he said. He came in. Marilyn was lying on the bed with the sheet pulled up to her chin.

I said, "Could you just fix her hair a little bit?"

"Yes, of course," he said, and he brushed her hair out with that magic touch.

"Okay," he said, straightening up. She really did look much better.

"Thanks a lot," I said.

I walked him to the door. As he left he turned and asked, "Do you need anything?"

"Well . . . we could use some more champagne," I said.

He went out and handed a fresh bottle through the door.

"Okay, thanks very much," I said. And I closed the door again.

I heard a giggle behind me. I turned, Nikon in hand.

Now she was really ready. She felt pretty again.

I filled her champagne glass beside the bed and stepped back to watch her through the camera.

She reached down for the glass. Her leg flew up, and the sheet came flying off. "Oops!" she giggled as she fell toward the floor, one hand on the champagne glass, the other clutching the sheets. *Blam* . . . I shot. She looked up and took a drink of champagne. *Blam!* I couldn't resist shooting. She looked at me strangely, as if she was wondering just what I had in my mind. And what *did* I have in mind? Nothing but the pure magic of this moment. I couldn't speak, I was so excited. *Blam!*

She was rolling all around the bed, and I was shooting. *Blang. Blang. Click. Click.* There was no time to check exposures, it was all happening so fast. Somehow she crawled on top of the sheet. I said, "Why don't you lie so that nothing shows?"

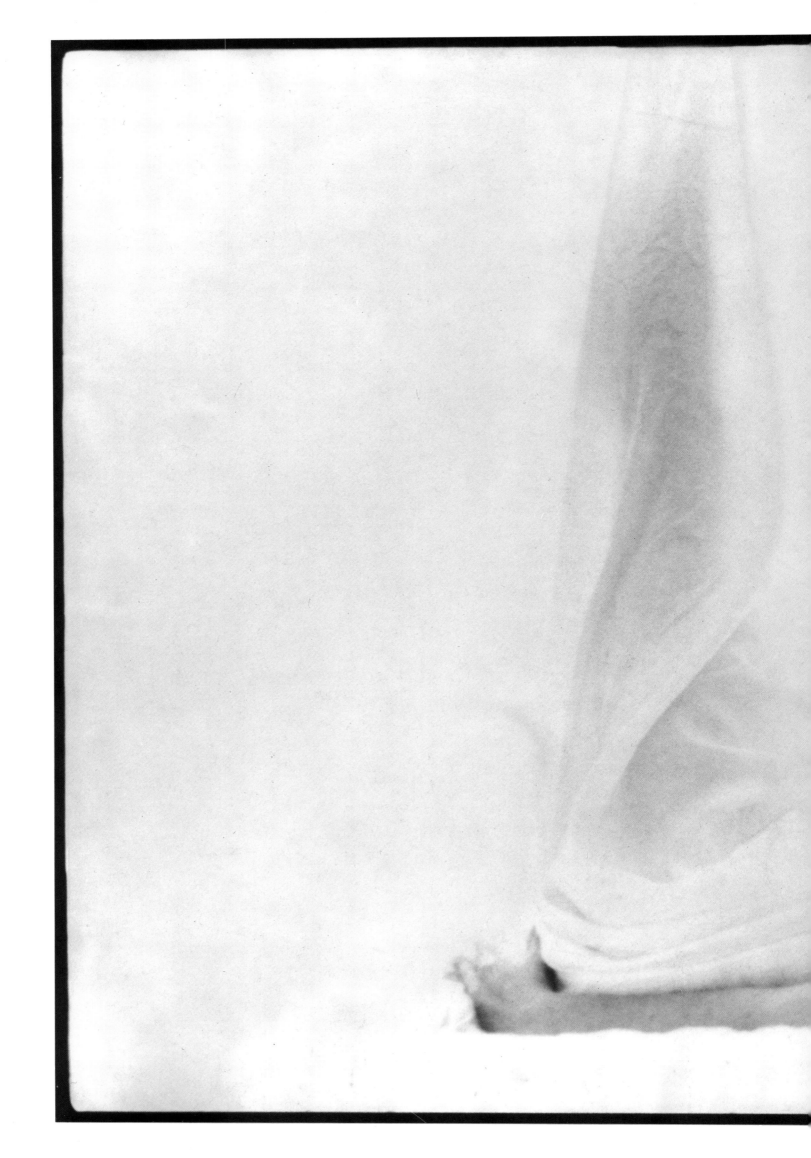

"How?"

"Well, if you hang one foot off the bed, I can only see your back."

"I need another glass of champagne," she said.

What I wanted was a totally stark clean beautiful nude—no clothes, nothing between her and me but the air. We were moving there . . . getting closer. *Blang* . . . I moved closer . . . *blang* . . . closer . . .

I was standing right above her.

But I didn't make that last step, where vision dissolves into touch. Not yet. If I did what I wanted to do now, it would be over too soon, and the energy that was creating the pictures would dissolve—fffft! So instead of reaching for her, which was what I wanted to do, I stayed right on the edge, at a magnetic distance that was like the opposite of touching. I wanted to take the time to dwell on the sight of her, and not go past.

That *energy of observing* is marvelous. When you desire someone so much, and she's right there in front of you, there's something very special about *not* touching, and just letting *the light* caress her. And the camera plays a very powerful role in all this. Because you've got love coming through the lens. You just let it in and click! Close the box, and you've recorded impressions of that love, that energy, in photographs you can print and preserve.

Ours is the first age that has been able to do that. There are no photographs of Cleopatra, no prints of what Paris saw and felt when he gazed at Helen of Troy. They're like dead stars: The light from them no longer reaches us. But there *are* photographs of Marilyn Monroe. The *same* light that touched her passed through the lens of a camera, leaving these pictures of her.

I stood beside her bed looking down at her, so close I could feel the heat of her skin. I didn't know whether to be her photographer, or to hold her. Since I was thirteen, I had dreamed of a woman who would roll around on a bed with me and do everything I ever wanted. Now I had found that woman. She was vulnerable and drunk and tender and inviting and exciting. But I had a camera in my hands and a drug in my veins.

My mouth was dry. My desire all seemed to be drawn up into my head and my eyes. I just kept going into that desire, expanding that space, making it brighter and brighter and brighter. The shutter feverishly clicked and whirred. In the whole world there were only the two of us, a man and a woman, alone together in that magical space of flashing white light.

How long were we out of this world? Gradually the intensity subsided. Marilyn looked at me with a sleepy intimacy. I captured that look. The flashing of the strobes got slower.

The flashes stopped.

She was quiet, her eyes closed.

She was mine . . . alone, all mine. What was I going to do next? Take off all my clothes and get into bed with her? With all those people sitting out there waiting for us?

Come on, Bert, whispered my demon. *The greatest opportunity any man could ever dream of, and it's right in the palm of your hand! You'll never have this chance again.*

No. I didn't want Marilyn Monroe this way.

It was late; Babs, Kenneth, and Peter were waiting patiently in the other room. Or had they gone home? I wasn't about to open that door and see. They were probably still out there, tapping their feet, or maybe half asleep. How long had it been? Ten minutes? Twenty?

My half a Dexedrine was beginning to wear thin, and I could feel fatigue creeping up. There was no reason to take any more pictures. I had shot everything I could.

Marilyn moved a little. I sat down on the bed next to her. I could hear her breathing. At least she's alive, I thought. I looked at her. She was just lying there beside me, peacefully, her eyes closed.

Or was she?

Maybe she was just waiting for me to . . . after all, why had she lifted up the veil and let me throw everybody out of the room? She had been in the mood for *something*.

But what?

Maybe I should kiss her. Why not?

I leaned over her . . .

As my lips touched her, she turned slightly away.

"No," she said.

My heart sank. I felt defeated.

But Marilyn didn't move. She didn't scream. She didn't sit up and slap me. She just crept back into her trance. I told myself all I had wanted was to pay tribute to the goddess of love on the altar of her lips. I cared about her enough to kiss her.

Of course there were other thoughts. Maybe all I was doing was trying to make a dumb pass at her, and not getting very far.

I sat there trying to feel better.

But, if she'd been insulted, wouldn't she just get up and leave? She didn't want to *kiss* . . . but maybe she wanted to make love.

I put my hand under the sheet and touched her skin.

The room stopped moving. Everything became silent.

She nestled closer.

The energy between us was pure magic. We were inches away from pure erotic pleasure.

She wanted to make love.

She was ready.

I was the one who stopped.

Why?

I've asked myself that question many times, and I've come up with many answers: marriage . . . prudence . . . cowardice . . . destiny . . . Dexedrine . . . But at that moment I think the truest one was that I cared

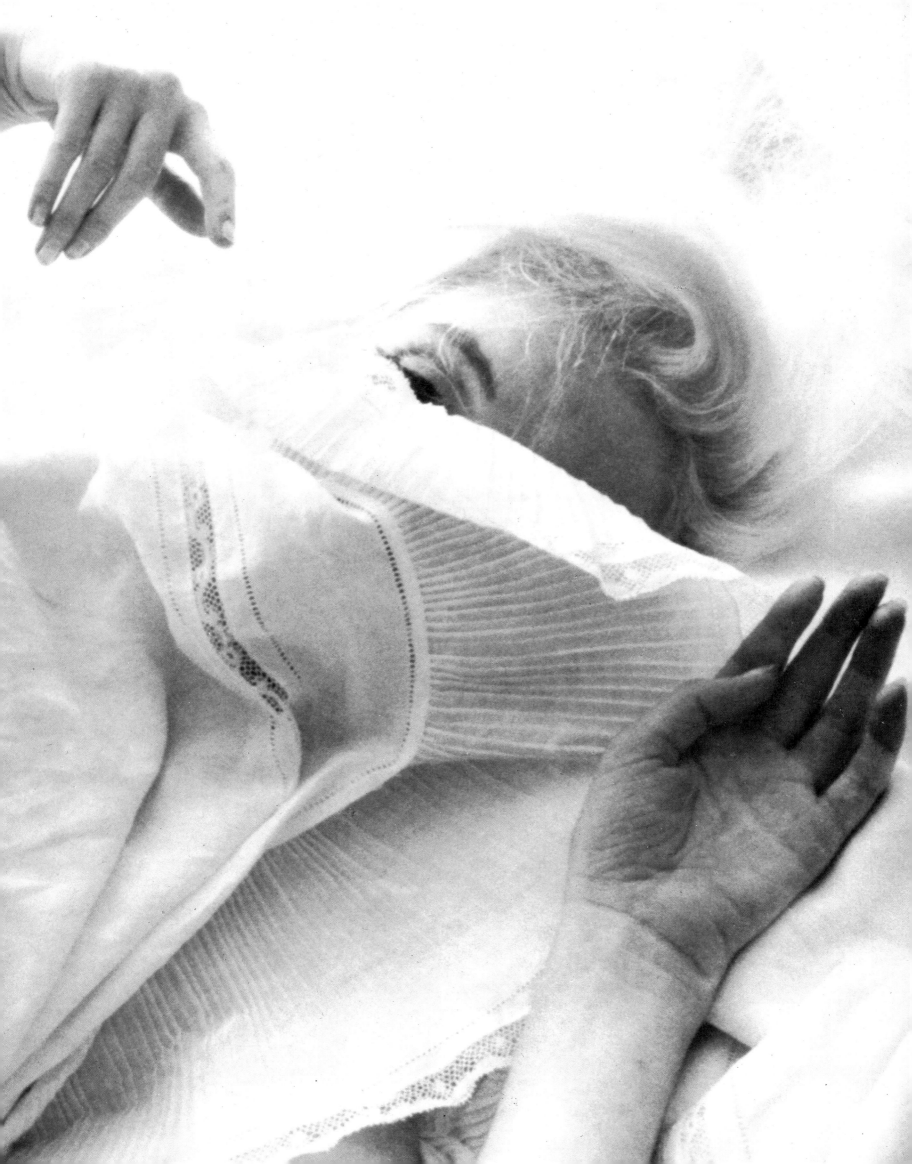

too much for her. My desire for Marilyn was pure, it bordered on awe. To make love to her would have been too much . . . and not enough.

Slowly I withdrew my hand.

Marilyn's eyes half opened and she stretched. She looked up at me, and said:

"Where have *you* been so long?"

Those were her last words to me that night.

So long.

And then she was asleep.

It was Sleeping Beauty in reverse. The prince was supposed to wake her up, not put her to sleep.

I stood up and picked up my camera. One more picture. The lighting was all wrong, and I didn't have the foggiest notion of what the exposure was. It wasn't even a good picture. But I had touched one of the sweetest of God's creatures and it seemed right to take one last shot of her.

I wanted her profile against the pillow. The only way to get that was to stand over her. I climbed up on the bed in my stocking feet. The shutter softly went click.

She didn't stir.

I stepped down off the bed and looked around the room. It looked like a bomb had hit it. Champagne bottles all over the place . . . her shoes in one corner . . . a bottle of Château Lafite '55 on its side . . . a half-empty glass still standing.

I carefully opened the door.

Everybody was still sitting there, half asleep. They looked at me. I closed the door softly.

"Well," I said, "I'm finished. She's asleep," I added. "I'm going for a walk."

And I left the bungalow.

The east was just beginning to get light. The night was cool and blue-black, and the tiny stars seemed even farther away than usual. I walked slowly around the bungalow. I wasn't happy, I wasn't depressed. I felt detached.

I walked around the corner of the bungalow. And there, behind the bedroom where I had left Marilyn asleep, were two Japanese cooks in their tall cook hats peering through the window. I had pulled down the shade in the studio so that the window was blacked out, but there was still a crack where light streamed through.

What a story they could have told if we had made love! As it was, they'd seen enough. I'd gone right up to the edge with her.

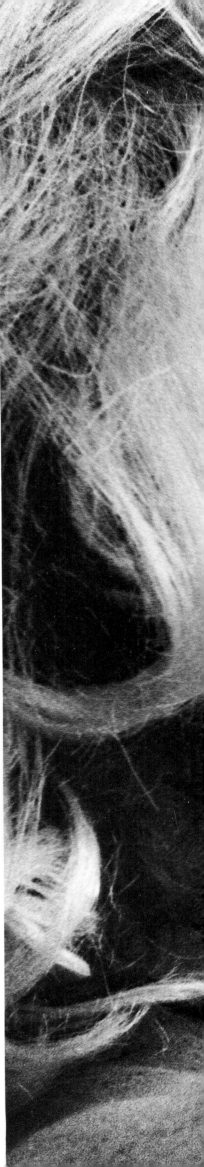

The next day she didn't show up. Late in the morning, Babs told me that Pat Newcomb had called and said Marilyn wasn't going to work today.

Why not? Had I gone too far with her? I immediately began to imagine all kinds of crazy things.

Then I wondered whether she was all right. She must have had quite a hangover. All that champagne and vodka . . . It wouldn't be at all surprising if she didn't feel like working today. That was probably it.

Then the phone rang again.

It was Pat Newcomb, asking whether Babs and Kenneth would come over to Marilyn's house at one o'clock. I wasn't invited. So Kenneth and Babs went off leaving me sitting there in the Bel-Air Hotel. I didn't feel great that day.

The two sittings had gotten gradually more and more intimate. It was building to something. Then all of a sudden I was nowhere. What had happened?

Peter and I cleaned up the mess in the studio, organized all the film I'd shot, and got things ready just in case there was going to be a shoot the next day. The rest of the afternoon was sunny and boring. Without Marilyn everything seemed to stand still. There was nothing for me to do but sit around and imagine the worst. I couldn't help thinking about what was going on over at Marilyn's house.

Maybe it had nothing to do with me. Maybe she had some kind of appointment or a date that night and wanted to get made up and wanted her hair done. Otherwise why would she have requested the editor and the hairdresser? Then there was the other possibility and that one seemed a lot more likely to me. The one where she's telling them all the terrible things I said and did to her. At this very moment she was probably saying, "I'll never work with that photographer again." Or worse, she could be making a big joke out of it. They were probably having a good laugh. At my expense.

What did I feel so guilty about?

My desires? What else?

I was a true child of the forties and fifties, those sexual dark ages. So was Marilyn, but Marilyn was a little bit ahead of her time. She had been called a sex symbol, as if that was something to be ashamed of, and her response was, "I'd rather be a symbol for sex than for some of the other things people are symbols for." Sex wasn't a dirty word for her. It still *was* for me.

And those nagging thoughts kept popping up. Why hadn't she shown up? Why hadn't I been invited?

Well, Bert, I said to myself, stop torturing yourself. You've shot a carload of unique shots of the most glamorous star on earth at her earthiest and most glamorous. Isn't that enough? Forget your fantasies about Marilyn. You were probably deluding yourself, anyway.

And then Babs came back and said, "She'll be here tomorrow."

When she came in for the third shooting, everything was very different. Especially Marilyn and me. Sober, subdued, not very talkative. There was nothing to say. And then there were all these people around us again: Kenneth, Babs, Pat Newcomb, Peter Deal.

We took some pictures outdoors, casual black and whites. I gave her my camera, and she took my picture. I took a picture of her holding the camera. We kidded around. But there was a distance there. You could feel it.

And then all of a sudden I remembered that I still hadn't done the picture I'd come for—that one black and white that was going to last forever, like Steichen's Garbo.

"I want to do one more picture," I said. "A beautiful head shot." Babs said, "Oh wonderful! We could use a great beauty shot. Kenneth will do the hair." Everybody was very excited.

I knew how I wanted to do it. One day when I was taking pictures of a girl, she said, "What should I do?" On an impulse I said, "Lie down." She said, "Okay," and I took her picture standing over her. It's very sexy that way, because the girl lying down feels receptive and pretty, and the photographer is in a position of power.

I was going to do one of those pictures of Marilyn. But I wasn't going to do it just standing over her with a wide-angle lens, because you get distortion using a wide-angle right up close. Telephoto would give a perfect close-up without distortion. But I would have to get way up high, on a ladder or something. I'd be moving away to get closer . . . using distance to capture the intimacy I would have had with her if things had been—different.

I built up a kind of scaffolding out of a table and a chair and I climbed up on it. The proportion still wasn't right; it needed more height. I added another chair. I had to be directly above her. I wanted her looking straight up into the eye of the beholder. As if he were making love to her. Whoever looked at this image of Marilyn would be stricken the way I had been. And she would give him back her love in that look. And they would be together for all time . . . it would be a picture of what might have been.

Everybody was working: Kenneth combing Marilyn's hair, Babs arranging a string of pearls around her neck. I was way up there in the dark, looking down on her lying there with her hair spread out.

Marilyn was a little pensive, and I wanted her laughing, alive. So I said, "Could someone turn her on, please?"

Babs offered her some champagne.

"No, no," I called down. "She can't move out of that position. Talk to her. Pat, talk to her."

Pat said to Marilyn, "What about those two loves in your life?"

Marilyn started to giggle.

I didn't know who Marilyn's lovers were but she obviously enjoyed thinking about them. She was laughing, looking over at Pat, and I said, "That's great! But look up here, at the camera." And to draw her attention to me, I said, "How *about* those two men . . . "

She was on, and the strobes were clicking, and the light was bouncing around, tinkling down, Kenneth came over with a handful of sparkle and scattered it in her hair. The pearls were around her neck, and she was laughing, free. And I whispered to myself, "Boy . . . how far out . . ." I really *had* her. The light was just right. Everything began to move a little faster.

It was coming—the moment I was looking for.

A lot of pictures I take are not the real picture. They're the picture

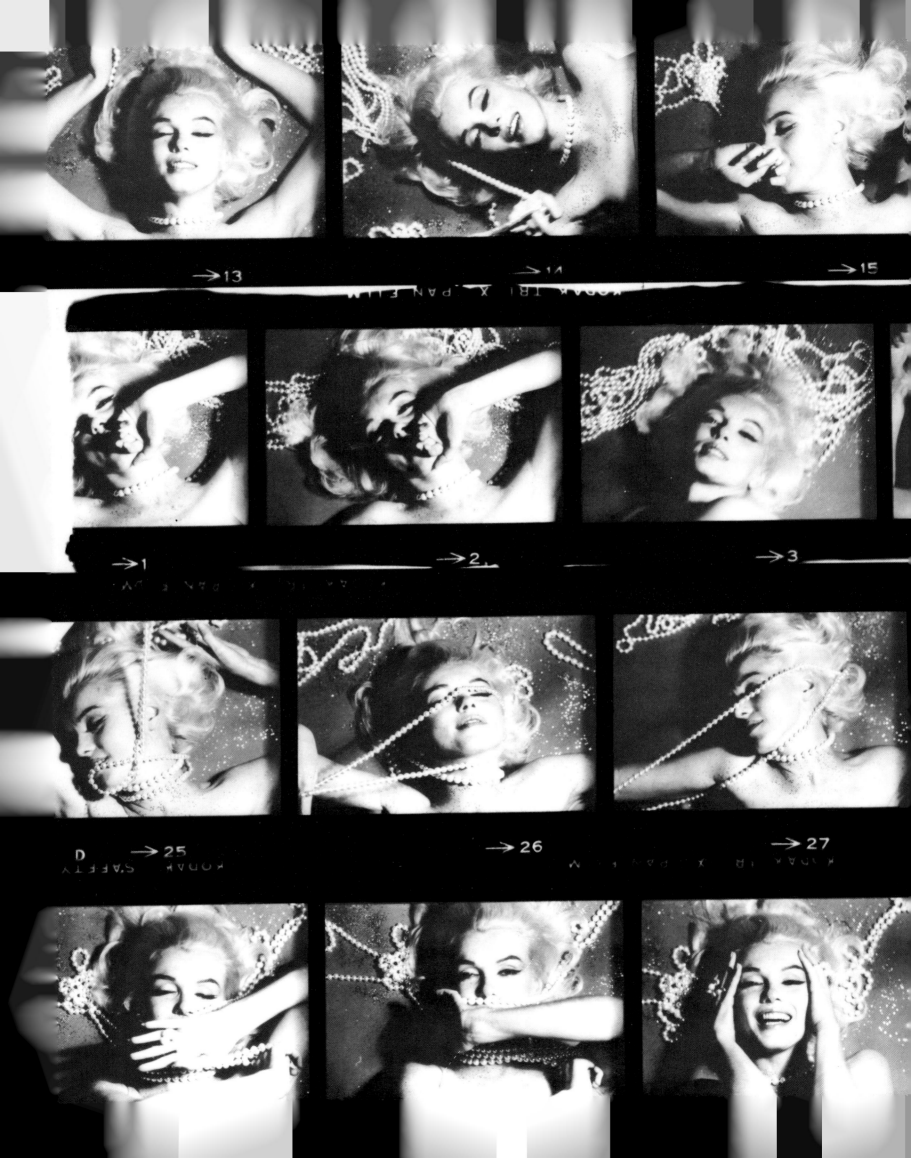

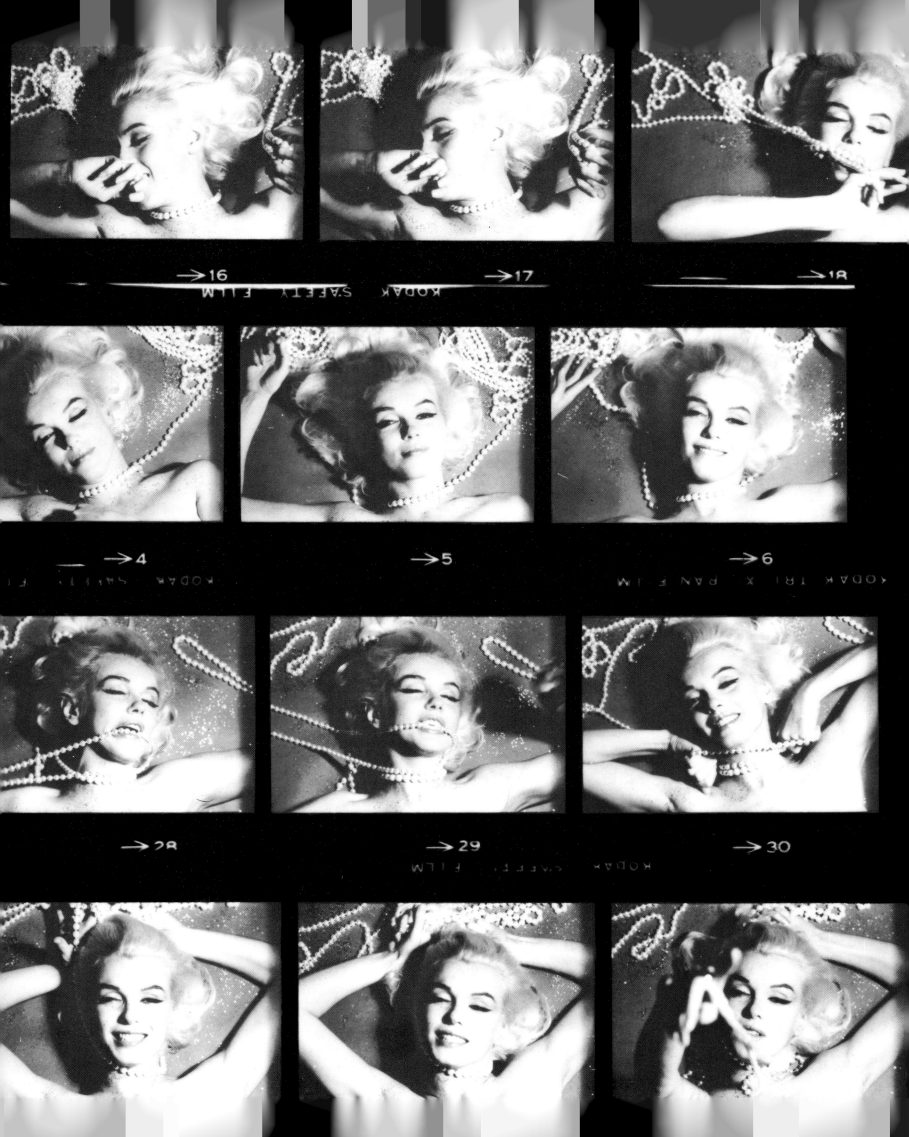

before the picture, the picture leading up to the picture—and then I get *the* picture. I see it through the lens as I'm shooting and I know it's the one. Exactly how I see it depends on the camera. On the Nikon and the Hasselblad you're looking right through the lens, so the shutter goes black when the actual picture is taken. On those cameras I don't see the picture itself. I keep shooting right up to that instant when I feel, I know, it's about to happen. Then I push the button and on that black space I project the picture. The Rolleiflex doesn't do that, because it has a twin lens. But then you don't see the actual picture either, because you're seeing through the upper lens, and the angle's slightly different.

Either way, you never see the picture that you're taking. At that perfect moment you just have to close your eyes and jump. And when that moment comes, it's a zillionth of a second. It will never be repeated again, it could take all eternity to get it back. You have to grab it.

Looking down on Marilyn, I could see it happening. I was entering that space where everything is silent but the clicking of the strobes. She was tossing her head, laughing, and her arm was up, like waving good-bye.

I saw what I wanted, I pressed the button, and she was mine.

It was the last picture.

"Okay, I got it," I said, and I climbed down. It was all over. Marilyn left with Pat Newcomb, and we all packed up and got ready to leave.

As we were leaving, Babs Simpson said, "What's going to happen to that poor girl?"

Poor girl?

I didn't quite see what Babs meant. I didn't feel sorry for Marilyn. I just figured I had done the best I could. And now I was going home.

I was a lucky guy: I had a home to go home to. In that respect, I knew, I was happier than Marilyn. I could look my wife straight in the eye if she asked me if I'd slept with Marilyn Monroe. It felt good to have a clear conscience. I was glad that it had turned out this way. Wasn't I?

My love affair with Marilyn had been photographic. It had all the energies a love affair should have and none of the problems. We had lived out the whole life of a great love in the span of three days: attraction, seduction, the big separation and the return, the making up and the final parting. We had come close, very close, to the real thing. And whatever I brought back, whatever is here, is the result of distilled desire.

If you want something, sometimes you've got to go right to the edge.

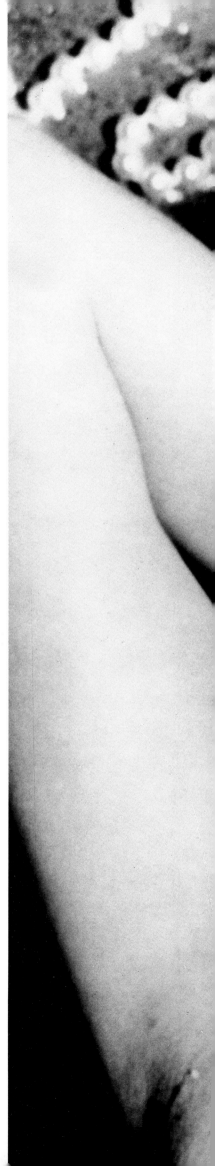

162

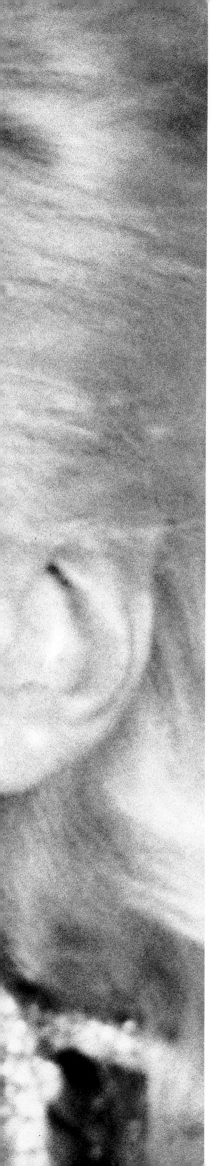

took the Red-Eye home, came into my house at dawn and kissed *my* Sleeping Beauty. This one woke up, smiled and said, "I love you." Our blond baby slept peacefully in the next room.

The next morning I went straight to my studio and into the lab. The jet stream of bubbles from the nitrogen burst reassured me that the development was in good hands. I told my darkroom man, Gar, that there were to be *no* mistakes, and to develop the film very slowly, one roll at a time if necessary. These were going to be the most gorgeous prints we had ever made.

Gar knew how to make prints the way I liked them, and I had built him the best darkroom setup money could buy. Not for color. Color was too complicated. It was technical—not a creative process, and it was better done outside in a color lab. But making a black-and-white print is an art. I shot in many tricky lighting setups and I could get the prints the way I wanted them only if the quality of the negatives was superlative. So I had spared no expense to make them that way. I'd spent about six thousand dollars just on sinks to develop the film in so that each negative would be perfect—sharp, clean, no dirt. Then Gar and I would work on a single print for hours or even days, making rough print after rough print until we were satisfied.

I had used some risky lighting with Marilyn and I knew it. There were some shots where I had turned the front light off and used just back-light. It was the only way I could get some feeling of illusion into the pictures. They were going to be the hardest to print. I could already see on the contact sheets which ones were going to be the most difficult, the most straightforward, the most beautiful. Slowly I began to pick out the prints of my own choice that I wanted to make up for *Vogue*, and Gar and I got to work.

On the third or fourth day we spent in the lab, Vickie buzzed me for a phone call. I shook the water off my hands and picked up the darkroom phone. "Hello?"

"Hello, Bert. How are the pictures?"

It was Pat Newcomb, calling from California.

"They're great," I said, cradling the phone between my shoulder and chin so I could check a print we'd just started. A ghostly image of Marilyn in chinchilla was beginning to materialize on the paper. "*Vogue* loves them."

"You know, don't you," said Pat, "that Marilyn has approval of all her photographs."

I realized that this was a call I had been expecting since the first day of this assignment. But they hadn't breathed a word of it until now. Approval had not been part of the deal, and even if they had asked for it, they almost certainly wouldn't have gotten it. I'd never known *Vogue* to grant photo approval to anyone, no matter how big a star.

"Look," I said. "It's one thing if I agree to give her approval, but I can't speak for *Vogue*. They're going to use whatever they want."

"She'd like to see all the pictures anyway," Pat said.

Marilyn gazed wistfully up at me from the developing tray. Her lips looked pale in the red light.

"Well . . . all right," I said. "I don't have the new ones back from the lab yet, but I'll send her the ones from the first shoot." I already knew *Vogue* wasn't going to use most of the nudes, so they'd probably give them back to me. "But send them right back, Pat, please."

She said, "Don't worry. We'll send all of them back."

The next day Gar and I had finished about thirty prints that I liked well enough to show. There were a lot of different grades. Some were perfectly good prints after only two or three hours work, but I still stamped them ROUGH, because I wanted *Vogue* to know that I would go back and make them even better. Others had really been worked on for days, especially the backlight shots. I put them all in a big envelope with all the contact sheets and went up to see Alex again.

I could have just sent them over, because I knew he was going to pick them anyway, but this time there was one picture I really cared about. It was that one head shot, the one I felt fulfilled my original assignment . . . the last picture I took. And I knew that if I didn't make a point of it, Alex might not pick it.

"This is my best shot," I said to him.

"Beautiful," he said.

I said, "I don't care what other pictures you use if you use this one."

He said, "We'll try to use it. They're all beautiful."

I tried again. "This one is the one I *really* want you to use!"

Alex nodded. "This one we will use," he said firmly.

It was done. I had the one picture that I wanted most in *Vogue*. Of course, they'd do anything they wanted with the rest of it, but that was fair.

As I left I asked Alex for some of the color nudes to send to Marilyn, and he gave me an envelope full of transparencies. I took them back to the studio and divided them into three piles. I had decided not to send her all of them, because they were originals, one of a kind, and I wasn't sure I'd get them back, or they could get lost in the mail. So I sent her just the first pile, one third of the color, and all the black-and-white contact sheets, because I had negatives for those.

Then I waited. To hear from Marilyn, to hear from *Vogue*. I went on to other jobs, but every once in a while I wondered what they were up to at *Vogue*. A week passed, then another week, and I didn't hear a word. They didn't call me in to show me what they were doing or to ask whether I liked it. Finally I thought, well, they *must* have finished those layouts by now. I'm going to call them.

I called the art department and got Alex's assistant.

"Hi, Bert! How are you? We haven't seen much of you lately."

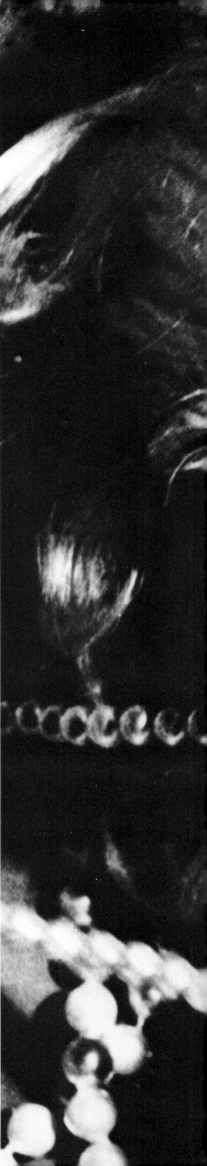

"Right," I said. "I was wondering about the Marilyn Monroe layouts. Do you suppose I could talk to . . ."

I could never get a call through to Alex's office when he was in there with the art editor and the editor-in-chief, making life-and-death decisions about pictures. "They can't come to the phone right now. As a matter of fact, they're in a meeting discussing your layouts. But don't worry, everything is wonderful. Alex says the layouts are beautiful."

"Well, thanks," I said. I hung up, shrugged, and went downstairs to get the mail.

"Looks like something here from Marilyn Monroe," Vickie said cheerfully.

She handed me a fat manila envelope; Marilyn had returned the pictures after all! I took the envelope upstairs and shook it out on my desk, just to make sure.

The pictures were all there, all right—but *she had crossed over half of them out.*

On the contact sheets she had made x's in magic marker. That was all right, although I didn't agree with her—I thought some of the ones she'd crossed out were beautiful. But she had x-ed out the color transparencies with a hairpin, right on the film. The ones she had x-ed out were mutilated. Destroyed.

I have to admit I felt some anger at her at that moment. Not that she didn't like all my pictures, but she'd been so destructive about it! Why couldn't she have picked up the phone and said, "Let's go over these together"?

There were a few she'd obviously crossed out because she had her eyeliner on crooked. That wasn't impossible to retouch. I could have told her if she'd asked me. Sure, her image was important to her, but it was important to me, too, and I would have been kinder to her. She hadn't just scratched out my pictures, she'd scratched out herself.

When she made her mark on these pictures, she had less than two weeks to live.

The next time I saw her was on a wall at *Vogue.*

They finally called me. Priscilla Peck, the art director of *Vogue,* said, "Bert, the layouts are finished. You should come over and look at the boards."

At last, the invitation I'd been waiting for.

"How do they look?" I asked.

"There's something very nostalgic and sad about them," she said. "Come take a look."

"Be right over."

I walked over to *Vogue* and went up to the art department. Priscilla took me into the room where the layouts were on the wall.

It was very different from what I had imagined.

They had done the whole section in black and white. No color. Not

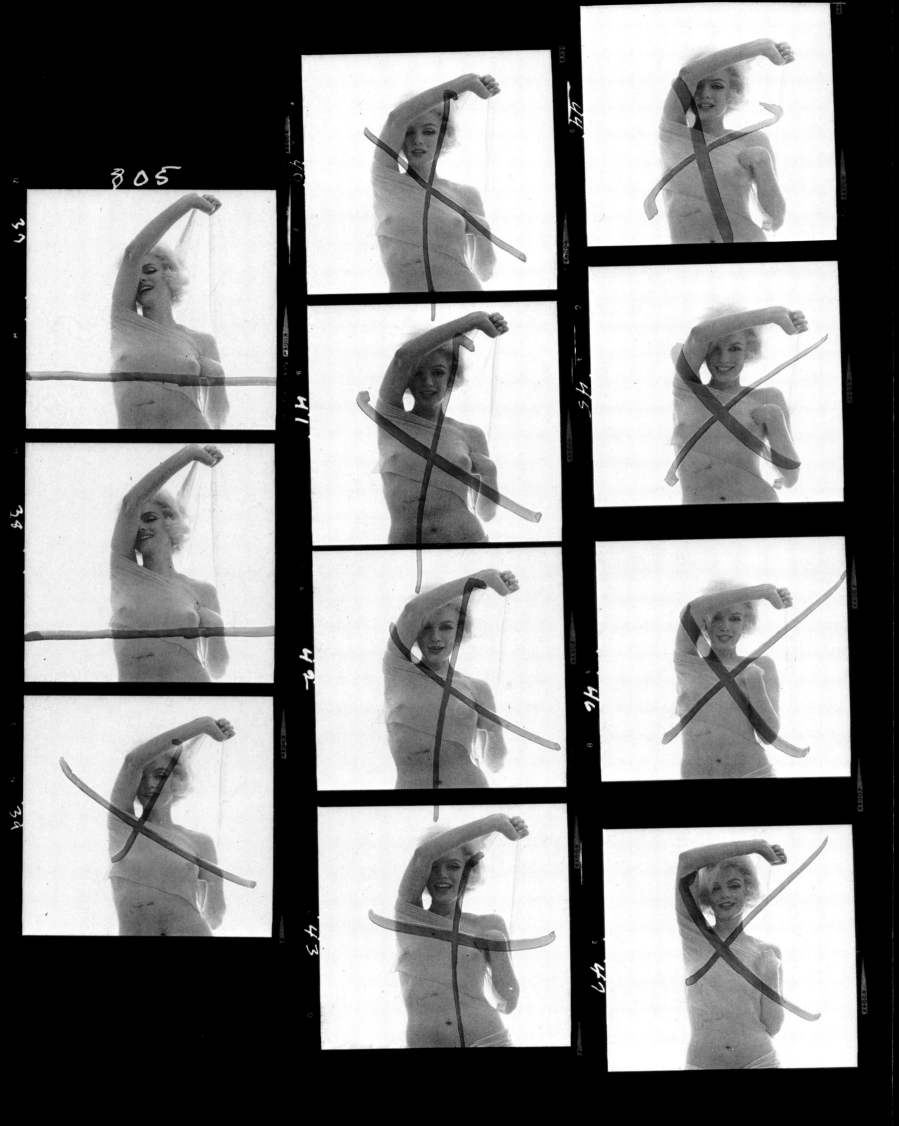

one of those hundreds and hundreds of beautiful nudes. They hadn't even used the black and white of the chinchilla with her bare leg showing, and I wondered why.

Vogue wasn't exactly conservative. They had run some marvelous nudes over the years. But maybe Marilyn was controversial—too sexy, too spicy. Maybe they felt it was better to cover her up in *Vogue.*

It was true, there *was* something haunting about the pictures they had chosen. All those black dresses, dark clothing, dark backgrounds . . . the layouts had an elegiac quality. It was strange and eerie.

Because Marilyn was still alive.

"Well, I guess it's all right," I said. At *Vogue* I was careful not to complain unless there was a good reason, because there were times when I had complained and they'd taken something out, and it ruined the section. And this one wasn't bad. At least they'd given her eight pages, and the last one was the laughing one I loved.

And all those color pictures from the first time were mine.

"It's fine," I said.

And so the pictures went to press, and I went home. Allegra was going off to dance somewhere, so I had to take our two-year-old, Trista, for the weekend. I put her in a big basket in the back seat of the car and drove out to Sag Harbor to visit some friends. That was Friday.

Saturday, August 4, I had a wonderful time. My pictures were safely in *Vogue,* so I could forget all about it and play on the grass with Trista and the other children. I only thought of Marilyn once. I was taking snapshots of Trista in one of those playpens made of netting, and I kept focusing on the mesh, and Trista had blond curls, and suddenly I thought, This is like Marilyn with the veil. It seemed like an interesting photographic parallel. Then the thought was gone and the long, sunny, carefree afternoon went on.

Sunday morning I had an invitation for brunch from other friends over on the beach side of the island. As I drove across from Sag Harbor to East Hampton, I was thinking, Boy, what a life. The sun was shining, and it was just ten miles of bliss. I drove up to the beautiful house my friends had rented and pulled into a circular gravel driveway, just like California. My feet crunched on the gravel as I walked to the door.

Inside, I noticed that there was a television on in the hallway, some morning show, just background noise. Then suddenly the announcer said, "We interrupt this program to bring you a special bulletin. Marilyn Monroe committed suicide last night."

I just stood there.

I didn't know *what* I felt. There seemed to be so many pieces of different feelings that I didn't know how to put them together. I was just paralyzed, shocked in a dumb, numb way. It was a strange reaction. I couldn't cry for Marilyn. There was some way in which I was not surprised. Not that she'd seemed depressed or suicidal to me. Not at all. It was more like

I'd smelled trouble. Or she *was* trouble.

And trouble begets trouble.

Babs had sensed it. *"What's going to happen to that poor girl?"*

And *Vogue* had laid her out in black.

Those layouts were on the press right now, ready to run. They were supposed to print the book on Monday. But they couldn't run that section now. Eight fashion pages would be inappropriate.

What was going to happen to the pictures now?

When I got in early Monday morning, the studio was buzzing. *Vogue* had already called. They had stopped the presses and they were having an emergency meeting. They only had a couple of hours to decide what to do. At first they all agreed that there was no way they could let it run. And then someone said, no, the pictures are beautiful. Why don't we just pull the fashion copy and print something special on the first page?

So they left the section just as it was. They didn't change one part of the layout. The pictures became a memorial—*Vogue's* salute to Marilyn, ending with the portrait of her laughing—the picture that goes back to the beginning, the one I set out to get.

That's the story of Marilyn Monroe and the photographer. I go on, and she says " . . . So long." It's the end of her career, and of her life, and in a sense it's the beginning of mine.

It was right after that that my greatest success as a photographer began. The kid from Brooklyn who was content with a job, a girl, a car, and a camera—the successful but clean-cut professional of 1962, was soon to metamorphose into the frenetic emperor of a seven-story studio where often ad and fashion shootings had to be set up simultaneously, where TV commercials were produced, and a small silk-screen factory was turning out limited editions of my work daily.

The sixties were to be the best and craziest decade, not only of America's life but of mine. Those were the years of the juke box, and the big sound, and the big bucks, and the swimming pool, and three children, and the townhouse, and the houseboy, the black library with the Picasso over the door, Dr. Feelgood, and the crystal blue Stingray, airplane trips to Fire Island, and the fantasy house with the wishing well, the herb garden, and the eight-foot-tall roses Allegra grew while I photographed American beauties in New York.

In 1962 I had these years of success and excitement still ahead of me and I also had yet to make my grandest mistakes. In a sense the taking of Marilyn's pictures was only a forewarning of things to come.

I know that in some way her spirit has been around me since then. Her pictures cut through a lot of obstacles on my way up and they got me out of some rough waters when I was down.

And as the years went by I noticed that the pictures we made together belonged to everybody. What I'd done was bigger than me. In one way or another they've passed out of my hands and into everyone's dreams. Some of the negatives have been lost or stolen. A whole envelope full of color transparencies was taken from my apartment in a robbery, and they reappeared on a construction site . . . where else but in Brooklyn? Marilyn peeks out from behind a scarf in the window of almost every poster and litho store.

So the pictures are everywhere. Marilyn is everywhere. But there *is* no Marilyn. She's gone. Marilyn was, as she said herself, a sex symbol. She died young and remains eternally young, a symbol preserved by death.

There have been many beautiful women since Marilyn Monroe. But who is there that has her total magic? Nobody has that vulnerability any more. We turn to child models in an instinctive search for that innocence and freshness, but they don't have the deep feminine sexuality that came from Marilyn like light.

Marilyn Monroe is the first American goddess—our goddess of love. We created her just as much as she created herself. She arose in response to *our* sexual yearning and *our* spiritual awakening. She is gone, but she is everywhere. Stars die, but light goes on forever.

Through the magic of photography the light from Marilyn Monroe is still reaching us, still drawing us on, like moths to a flame.

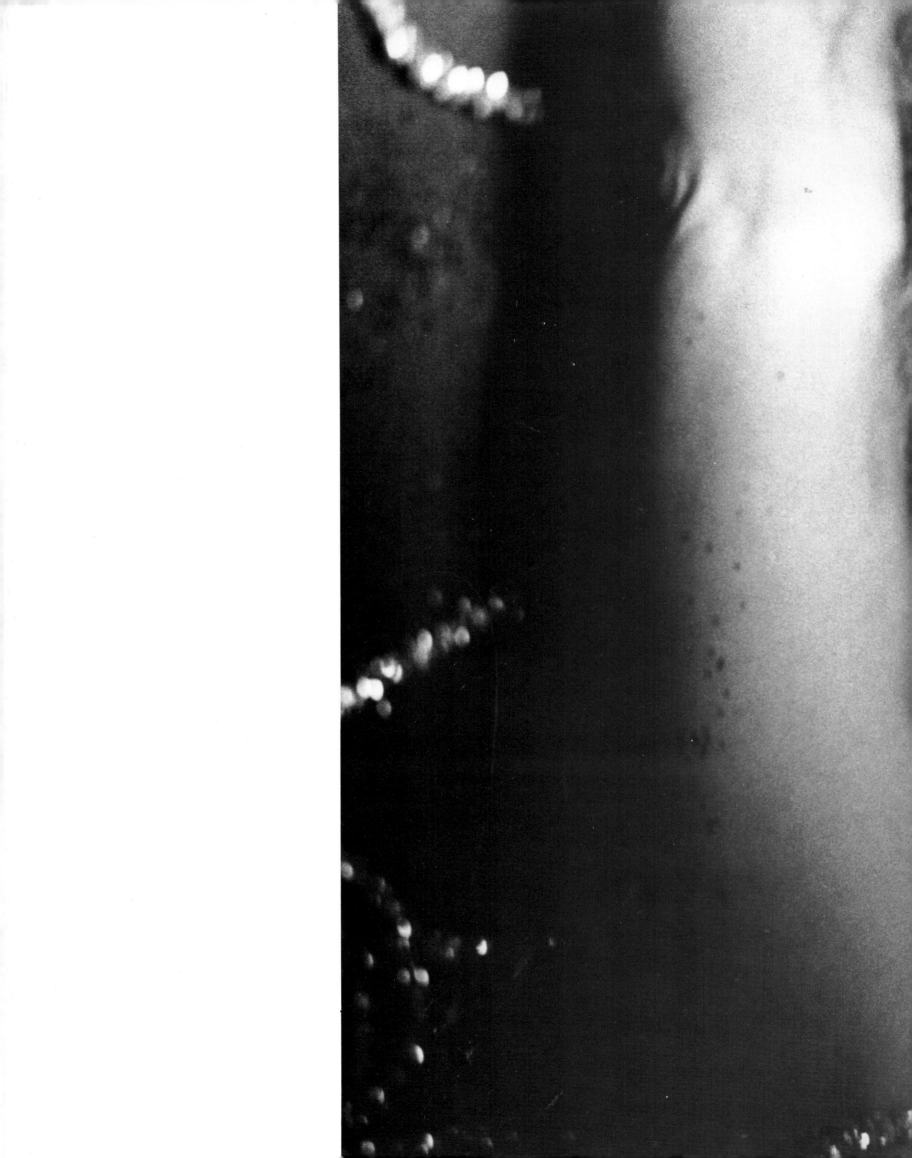

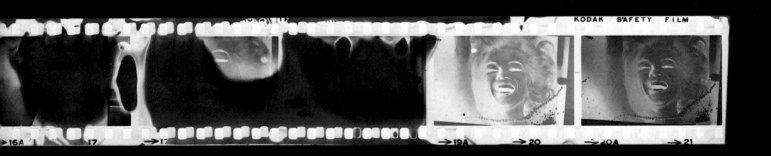